☀ INSIGHT COMPACT GUIDE

Salzburg

Compact Guide: Salzburg is the ultimate quick-reference guide to this historic Austrian city. It tells you all you need to know about Salzburg and the surrounding region, from the baroque splendour of the city's churches and monuments to the stunning alpine scenery just a short drive away.

This is one of 133 Compact Guides produced by the editors of Insight Guides, whose books have set the standard for visual travel guides since 1970. Packed with information, arranged in easy-to-follow routes, and lavishly illustrated with photographs, this book not only steers you round Salzburg and its province but also gives you fascinating insights into local life.

DISCOVERY
CHANNEL

APA PUBLICATIONS
Part of the Langenscheidt Publishing Group

Insight Compact Guide: Salzburg

Written by: Margret Sterneck
English version by: Paul Fletcher
Photography by: Britta Jaschinski/Apa
Additional photography by: Annabel Elston; John Spaull;
the Austrian Tourist Board
Cover picture by: Barry Mason/Alamy
Picture Editor: Hilary Genin
Maps: Franz Huber and Gert Oberländer/Lovell Johns

Editorial Director: Brian Bell
Managing Editor: Maria Lord

CONTACTING THE EDITORS: As every effort is made to provide accurate
information in this publication, we would appreciate it if readers would
call our attention to any errors and omissions by contacting:
Apa Publications, PO Box 7910, London SE1 1WE, England.
Fax: (44 20) 7403 0290; e-mail: insight@apaguide.co.uk

Information has been obtained from sources believed to be reliable,
but its accuracy and completeness, and the opinions based thereon,
are not guaranteed.

© 2006 APA Publications GmbH & Co. Verlag KG Singapore Branch, Singapore.

First Edition 1995; Second Edition 2006; Reprinted 2006
Printed in Singapore by Insight Print Services (Pte) Ltd
Original edition © Polyglott-Verlag Dr Bolte KG, Munich

Worldwide distribution enquiries:
APA Publications GmbH & Co. Verlag KG (Singapore Branch)
38 Joo Koon Road, Singapore 628990
Tel: (65) 6865-1600, Fax: (65) 6861-6438

Distributed in the UK & Ireland by:
GeoCenter International Ltd
Meridian House, Churchill Way West,
Basingstoke, Hampshire RG21 6YR
Fax: (44) 1256 817988

Distributed in the United States by:
Langenscheidt Publishers, Inc.
36-36 33rd Street 4th Floor
Long Island City, New York 11106

www.insightguides.com

Introduction

Places

Culture

Travel Tips

△ **Pacher Alter (p56)** Created by Michael Pacher, the altar (1471–81) at the church of St Wolfgang's is a masterpiece of late Gothic art and the church's most important work of art.

△ **Hohensalzburg Fortress (p22)** Perched high on a rock and dominating the city below, is the town's spectacular 15th-century fortress.

◁ **Mozart's Birthplace (p32)** A pilgrimage site for fans, Mozart's birthplace is on one of the city's oldest streets, the Getreidegasse.

△ **Hallstatt's Prehistori Museum (p67)** Extensive finds have led to the early Iron Age (c800-400BC) being called the Hallstatt era. Many archaeological finds are now on display in the town's museum.

◁ **Mirabell Gardens (p37)** Remaining virtually unchanged since it was designed in 1730, the Mirabell Palace has beautiful gardens.

△ **Krimml Waterfall (p98)** The view of the River Ache cascading 380 m (1,264 ft) down the Salzach is a spectacular sight.

△ **The Cathedral** (p28) This 17th century cathedral became the model for many churches in the south German region.

Hellbrunn Palace (p41) The summer palace's main attraction, the Surprise Fountains, will delight children of all ages. The Stone Theatre and the Hellbrunn Zoo, also nearby, make this a good day trip.

△ **Residenzplatz (p26)** Marking the heart of the princely baroque capital this magnificent square has a Renaissance-style fountain.

▷ **Monastery of St Peter** (p30) Revealing traces of every architectural epoch since the 7th century, the oldest section of this extensive monastery complex are its catacombs.

The City of Mozart

Salzburg – the very name conjures up images of music festivals, dignified houses and baroque church towers, and of course, Mozart. 'Mozart simply had to be born here,' said the poet Hugo von Hofmannsthal – in the heart of Europe, at the geographical and cultural meeting-point between north and south, between mountain and plain, between rural and urban ways of life.

Salzburg is no longer the dreamy little place admired by the writers and artists who visited in the early 20th century. Nowadays there is a never-ending stream of tourists wandering through the heart of the historic Old Town, which is so carefully preserved that it has almost become an open-air museum. If you want to see more of Salzburg than the obligatory tourist circuit, allow plenty of time to explore its lesser-known charms.

THE PROVINCE AND ITS CAPITAL

The provincial capital of Salzburg shares its name with the federal land of the same name. The former seat of the Prince-Archbishops and its hinterland did not become part of Austria until the beginning of the 19th century. Salzburg province itself offers a wide variety of landscapes, from the gently rolling Flachgau and the lakes and mountains of the Salzkammergut district (which is shared with two other provinces) to the glacial regions of the Tauern Mountains. Salzburg is an ideal destination for a cultural sightseeing tour or for a longer, more restful stay.

Indeed, the very concept of a holiday was invented in the 19th century in the region's traditional recreational areas such as the Gastein Valley, Zell am See and the Salzkammergut, when noblemen and the prosperous middle classes fled from the heat of the city in summer to enjoy the cool country air. Many new destinations have of course established themselves since then: the High Tauern, the Amadé World of Sport and the region surrounding the Dachstein and the Tauern provide excellent winter sports facilities. The

City of Music
Salzburg cashes in on its most famous son throughout the year, but two festivals in particular celebrate his musical legacy: Mozart Week is held at the end of January every year, timed to mark the composer's birthday of 27 January. In July and August, during the Salzburg Festival, performances of his works are played at various venues throughout the city.

Opposite: fountain at Residenzplatz
Below: sightseers at the castle

High Tauern National Park, which includes the Grossglockner Road and the Krimml Waterfalls, appeals to nature lovers.

LOCATION AND SIZE

The Austrian province of Salzburg covers an area of 7,154 sq. km (2,760 sq. miles), which represents just over eight percent of the total land area of the country. To the north Salzburg is bordered by Upper Austria, to the east by Styria, to the south by Carinthia and East Tyrol and in the Krimmler Alps by South Tyrol. To the west the province is bordered by Tyrol and Bavaria.

Since ancient times the province itself has been subdivided into five *Gaue*, or districts. The Flachgau comprises the Salzburg Basin (part of the Alpine foothills) and the Salzburg section of the Salzkammergut, which makes up only a small part of the famous lake and mountain area *(see page 51)*. Nonetheless, since the Salzkammergut is so closely linked with the city of Salzburg in terms of its geography, transport infrastructure and tourism, this book continues into the adjoining areas of Upper Austria and Styria.

The area of the Salzach Valley between Hallein and Golling and the Tennengebirge mountains and the Lammertal was officially proclaimed an independent *Gau* in 1896. The Tennengau is the newest and also the smallest *Gau* in the federation. The Lungau is not much bigger; it is a high upland basin surrounded by lofty mountain chains. Its only opening is to the east, towards Styria. From Salzburg you can reach the Lungau via the Tauern motorway or via the Tauern Pass at Radstadt.

The area to the west is the Pongau, once famous for its gold deposits. Today, its inhabitants earn a living from tourism instead. Further to the west lies the Pinzgau, severed by the Salzach Valley which crosses the region from west to east. It includes the Saalach Valley as far as the national frontier in the north, and in the south, an area culminating in a chain of mountains, all of them over 3,000 m (9,600 ft) high. One of these great peaks, the Grossvenediger, is 3,675 m (11,760 ft) high.

The Grossglockner Road
The highest mountain in Austria, the Grossglockner (3,800 m/12,155 ft), in fact lies within the province of Carinthia, but the Pinzgau can console itself with the thought that the longest section of the famous Grossglockner Road lies within its boundaries.

Mirabell Palace

GEOLOGY

Geographically described as part of the Alpine foothills, the region is characterised by gently rounded hills which generally reach altitudes of no more than 1,000 m (3,200 ft). During the Quaternary era the Salzach glacier scoured out a number of basins, some of which later became filled with water to form lakes (the Trumer Lakes and the Wallersee).

The city's surrounding mountains (the Kapuzinerberg, Festungsberg, Mönchsberg, Rainberg and Hellbrunnerberg) rise from the floor of the Salzburg Basin, which gives way in the south to the limestone Alpine foothills. The latter still retain the characteristics of a low mountain range and include the Kammerker/Sonntagshorn mountains as well as the Rossfeld, Gaisberg, Osterhorn, Schafberg and Gamsfeld groups.

The limestone High Alps, by contrast, rise vertically from the valleys and often possess broad, undulating upland areas – such as the Untersberg, Reiteralm, Loferer and Leoganger Steinberge, Steinernes Meer, Hochkönig, Hagen-Gebirge, Hoher Göll, Tennengebirge and Dachstein ranges. Precipitation and melting ice and snow have scoured vertical karst chimneys and caves in the limestone mountains. The gorges of the Saalach Valley bear impressive witness to the power of water. In the Eisriesenwelt caves

Below: the lake by Leopoldskron Palace
Bottom: Grossglockner, Austria's highest mountain, in autumn

in the Tennengebirge and in the Dachstein Caves, the cold air in winter has frozen the seeping water into unusual shapes.

You will find countless pretty lakes not only in the Alpine foothills, but also in the valleys and at the foot of the high mountain ranges. These include the Attersee, Traunsee, Wolfgangsee, Hallstätter See and the beautiful Altausseer See.

The main valley of the Salzach divides the schistose region from the Central Alps. The water from the streams of the Tauern plunge down from the side valleys over high sills, the most dramatic of which form the Krimml Waterfalls. Over the millennia they have eroded breathtaking gorges, such as the Gastein Gorge, the Kitzloch Gorge and the Liechtenstein Gorge.

The Central Alps are made up of gneiss and slate. The High Tauern consists of a series of ranges including a number of peaks of more than 3,000 m (9,600 ft) high. The Venediger group has the largest number of glaciers. Under the precipitous slopes of the Grossglockner (3,797 m/ 12,150 ft), just outside the boundaries of Salzburg province, lies the Pasterze, the longest valley glacier in Austria. Gold was once mined here in the lower Sonnblick and Goldberg mountains.

Directly to the east, framed by the Enns and Mur valley, lie the Low Tauern. The first ranges

Grass Mountains
Between the limestone High Alps and the Central Alps lies a zone of schistose rock, also known as the *Grauwackenzone*. The gently rounded peaks are covered with soil which is ideal for pastures and grazing lands. These hills are sometimes referred to by the old Salzburg term 'Grass Mountains', while the limestone Alps are known as 'Stone Mountains'.

The atmospheric Wolfgangsee

are the Radstädter and Schladminger Tauern, which form the northern boundary of the Lungau Basin. Prehistoric glaciers have left behind numerous *Kars*, in which water then collected to form little lakes.

The southern boundary of the Lungau Basin is formed by the Gurktaler Alps, whose contours are gently rounded despite their height.

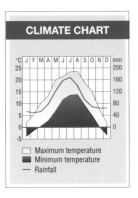

CLIMATE CHART

Maximum temperature
Minimum temperature
— Rainfall

CLIMATE

Salzburg province has a Central European transitional climate. The northern boundary of the Alps is damp and cool; the westerly and north-westerly winds from the Atlantic bring damp air masses which turn to rain or snow in the mountains. 'Salzburger Schnürlregen' is a local expression to describe this weather phenomenon. However, Salzburg is by no means the wettest region of Austria.

The alpine climate within the mountain area is characterised by short, relatively cool summers with long hours of sunshine, and long winters with plenty of snow. The Lungau has rather less precipitation; its high-altitude plateau, surrounded by mountain peaks, enjoys a continental climate with cold winters and short summers but plenty of sunshine all the year round. Mariapfarr is the sunniest spot in the entire country.

FLORA AND FAUNA

Encompassing the lowland marshes and river meadows of the Flachgau to the high-altitude pastures and glacial zones of the Pinzgau, the province of Salzburg contains a wide variety of habitats, each with its own distinctive flora and fauna. The number of nature trails is constantly increasing and along the way provide the walker with information about the wealth of species and characteristics in that particular region. In the High Tauern National Park you can also join nature walks led by naturalists who will be able to lead you into protected biotopes.

In summer, rare black and bearded vultures

Ibex inhabit the lower altitudes of the High Tauern National park

Föhn

This is an infamous weather condition that dominates Alpine regions for at least 45 days of the year. It signifies a strong, dry, warm wind and the lowering of humidity in the air. It brings sub-tropical weather in summer and pleasant spells in winter. This innocent sounding phenomenon is credited with the ability to lay low an entire city. Headaches and frayed nerves are common occurrences, while the incidence of suicides, crimes and traffic accidents increases.

In the High Tauern National Park

make their summer homes on the steep mountain slopes of the valleys of the Rauris and Hollersbach. Driving along the Grossglockner Road you will pass through several different climatic and topographical zones within the space of just a few hours: meadows, woodland, mountain pastures, dwarf pine forests, bare rocks and perpetual ice. Eagles, ibex, chamois, snow grouse, Arctic hares and marmots have their homes here at altitudes above 1,300 m (4,160 ft).

POPULATION

The province of Salzburg has 508,000 inhabitants, just under 6 percent of the total population of Austria, making it one of the smallest in the country, just above Burgenland and Vorarlberg. The city of Salzburg, however, has 140,000 inhabitants, and is the fourth largest city in the country after Vienna, Graz and Linz.

About one-tenth of the workforce are employed in agriculture and forestry, one-third work in industry and trade, while over half make a living in the service sector.

Some 80 percent of the population are Roman Catholic, just over 3 percent are Protestant and the rest are distributed between other religious groups and those of no fixed religious affiliation. There are very few Protestants in Austria today because during the Counter-Reformation they were persecuted and forced either to recant or emigrate.

Apart from Croatian, Slovenian, Hungarian and Czech minorities in the border regions, the people of Austria all speak German, although this does not necessarily mean that German speakers from further afield will understand everything they hear. There are small linguistic differences from one province to another and from one region to another within these provinces. Like all Austrian dialects except the Alemannic dialect spoken in the Vorarlberg, the German spoken in Salzburg belongs to the Bavarian-Austrian group.

CUSTOMS AND TRADITIONS

Most Alpine customs are heathen in origin and were integrated into the Christian year at a later date. They usually symbolise a prayer for fertility or the exorcism of evil spirits. In many villages in the Pinzgau and the Pongau, *Perchten* (ghosts) walk in procession through the streets on the Feast of the Epiphany. They personify good spirits (*Schönperchten*, dressed in light colours and adorned with jewels) or evil demons (*Schiachperchten*, with fearful wooden masks). In the Salzkammergut you will see attractive, glittering masks known as *Glöckler*. On the day before Shrove Tuesday in Bad Aussee, the *Trommelweiber* (women) run through the streets in friendly-looking masks, wearing nightcaps and nightgowns; on Shrove Tuesday itself it is the turn of the *Flinserl*, whose linen costumes are decorated with glittering silvery plates.

In the Lungau, the *Prangstangen* (poles up to 6 m (19 ft) long wound round with garlands of flowers) are carried into the church in a procession (in Zederhaus this takes place on 24 June while in Muhr festivities begin on 29 June). They remain there as a symbol of life itself until the Feast of the Assumption. In some villages in the Lungau (including Tamsweg, St Michael, Muhr, Ramingstein, Lessach and Mariapfarr), the Samson Procession is held on the Feast of Corpus

Below: pretzels for sale
Bottom: traditional costumier

Krampus

If you are in Austria during the week before 6 December, you will be able to witness the Krampus runs. Krampus is a tradition originating in pagan times, but incorporated into Christianity through time. The Krampus is a scary goat-horned creature that runs around beating the evil spirits out of naughty children (and adults) before the arrival of St Nicholas. The tradition thrives in Alpine Europe and in each region there are slight variations in the tales and customs associated with the Krampus. However, the common factor is that they are large and frightening. You will be alerted to their proximity by the sound of bells, so beware!

Christi or on a specific day in June or July. A tall wooden statue dressed in armour and a tunic is paraded through the streets. In his hand, the figure clutches the jawbone of an ass, with which Samson is said to have slewn the Philistine hordes. The origins of this ancient custom remain something of a mystery.

ECONOMY

Salzburg's economy is one of the most dynamic in Austria, with a typical post-industrial structure dominated by the service sector; industry accounts for about 30 percent of the economy, while agriculture, mining and energy production contribute about 4 percent. The economy is largely export-orientated. Inhabitants of Salzburg have a well above average income and unemployment is fairly low compared to other EU countries. Salzburg has a reputation as one of the best places to invest in Europe and the thriving tourism industry is set to expand even further.

Today fewer than one-third of the province's farmers rely exclusively on their farms for income; the large number of mountain farmers require massive subsidies from the state to survive. The dairy and cheese-making industries are only of great importance in the Flachgau.

Hallein is the most important industrial town

The river from the northwest

in Salzburg province. The Salzberg mine on the Dürrnberg which gave the city and province its name was closed down in 1989; however, it continues to make money as a tourist attraction. The Tauern power stations at Glockner-Kaprun are as impressive as they are efficient. Tourism, with a total of over 22 million overnight stays each year, is a major source of income to the region.

ADMINISTRATION AND POLITICS

The Republic of Austria is a federal state in which the nine constituent provinces each enjoy sovereign rights with regard to local government and legislation. The population of each province elects its provincial assembly every four years. In Salzburg Province, following the local elections in March 2004 the Social Democrats (SPÖ) have a majority of 17 members in the Regional Parliament, while the People's Party (ÖVP) have 14, the Freedom Party (FPÖ) have 3 and the Green Party have 2 members. In April 2004, the Salzburg Regional Parliament elected Gabi Burgstaller as Governor of the Province of Salzburg. This was a first for the Social Democrats and she is Salzburg's first female provincial governor. She is responsible for administration, education and training, science and research policy, health and hospitals as well as women's and equality matters. The chairman of the provincial government is also the provincial head of Salzburg province. In common with the other provinces of Austria, the Salzburger Land is subdivided into districts: Flachgau, Tennengau, Pinzgau, Pongau and Lungau, each with its own district councils responsible for local government.

Within the districts lie the individual communities with their own individual administrations. Among the 119 communities within Salzburg province there are 30 market towns and four municipal communities: Hallein, Radstadt, Zell am See and the provincial capital, Salzburg. The latter is also the seat of the provincial government, the district administration for Salzburg and surroundings, the city council and the mayor.

Below: no shortage of shopping opportunities
Bottom: lunch with a view

HISTORICAL HIGHLIGHTS

The first permanent settlement of the region occurred on the plains and on the Rainberg during the New Stone Age (4000–1800 BC). During the Bronze Age (1800–900 BC), Salzburg became the copper trading heart of Central Europe. During the Hallstatt era (800–400 BC), salt mining assumed prime importance. With the advent of the La Tène era (400 BC until the dawn of the Christian era), the Hallstatt salt mines were overtaken in importance by those on the Dürrnberg near Hallein, an area settled by Celts.

15BC The Celtic kingdom of Noricum, including Salzburg (Juvavum), becomes a province of the Roman Empire.

AD45 Three Roman roads meet at Salzburg and it acquires town status.

After 488 The Romans withdraw from the province of Noricum. In the 6th century, the Baiuvari (Bavarians) settle in the northern part of the plains. In the 7th century the Avars and Slavs advance to the Lungau in a bid to settle the Eastern Alpine area.

c696 Bishop Rupert of Worms is given land and the town of Salzburg. The Monastery of St Peter becomes a centre of missionary activity, a convent is built on the Nonnberg and the Maximilian Monastery in Bischofshofen is constructed.

739 Salzburg becomes a bishopric and in 774 the first cathedral is dedicated.

788 Charlemagne ends the Agilofing dynasty, which had played a major role in the rise of Salzburg. Ten years later Pope Leo III makes Abbot-Bishop Arno of Salzburg an archbishop at the request of Charlemagne.

9th century Salzburg becomes the hub of missionary activity reaching as far as the Plattensee.

955 Victory of Emperor Otto I against the Hungarians. Archbishop Herold of Salzburg takes part in a rebellion against Otto I and is sent into exile.

987–996 Work starts on the building of a large abbey church and the extension of the cathedral. Emperor Otto III awards Salzburg a town charter and the right to levy customs duties and mint its own coins.

c1077 Archbishop Gebhard intervenes in the Investiture Dispute. As protection against the imperial armies he commissions the fortresses of Hohensalzburg, Hohenwerfen and Friesach.

1166 During the conflict between Emperor Friedrich Barbarossa and the pope, Salzburg sides with the pope again. The emperor places an imperial ban on the city and it is reduced to ashes. In 1177 the Peace of Venice is concluded: Cardinal Konrad von Wittelsbach is appointed Archbishop of Salzburg. Work begins on the reconstruction of the cathedral.

c1190 Salt mining in Hallein is resumed, forming the basis for the prosperity and cultural ascendancy of Salzburg.

1328 Salzburg and surroundings declare independence from the alliance with the Duchy of Bavaria. Archbishop Frederick promulgates the first Salzburg provincial constitution.

1348–9 The plague kills around one-third of the city's population.

End of 14th century Under Archbishop Pilgrim II of Puchheim, Salzburg covers its maximum area and extends its influence. The first Golden Age of the gold mining industry in the Tauern.

1403–81 Salzburgers unite against the archbishop, but fail to assert their claims (eg for lower taxation). In 1481 Emperor Frederick III proclaims Salzburg to be a Free Imperial City, weakening the power of the archbishop.

1495–1519 Archbishop Leonhard von Keutschach re-establishes princely power and extends the fortress. In 1498 he expels Jews from the city. In 1511 the town council and the mayor are forced to give up rights awarded by Frederick in 1481.

1525–6 Salzburg becomes one of the arenas of the Peasants' War, a revolt against the upper classes.

1587–1612 Archbishop Wolf Dietrich von Raitenau remodels the town into a princely baroque city. In 1598 the cathedral is burned down. In 1612 Wolf Dietrich is forced to abdicate after a failed coup and dies in prison in Hohsalzburg Fortress in 1617.

1612–1732 Archbishop Marcus Sitticus rebuilds the cathedral (dedicated in 1628). Archbishop Paris Count Lodron founds the university in 1623. Johann Bernhard Fischer von Erlach erects a number of churches. The persecution of Protestants begins under Archbishop Leopold Anton Firmian.

1756 Wolfgang Amadeus Mozart is born in Salzburg on 27 January.

1800 The French army marches into Salzburg. In 1803 the Imperial Deputation Edict rescinds the clerical state.

Salzburg, now in secular hands, is ceded to Archduke Ferdinand III of Tuscany.

1816–1818 Salzburg joins the Archduchy of Austria. In 1818 fire destroys part of Salzburg. First performance of the carol *Silent Night* in the church of St Nikolaus, Oberndorf.

1861 Salzburg receives its first elected parliament and provincial government.

1914–20 The assassination of the heir to the Austrian throne, Franz Ferdinand, in Sarajevo, provokes World War I. After the collapse of the Danube Monarchy (1918), Salzburg becomes part of the Democratic Republic of Austria. The first performance of Hugo von Hofmannsthal's *Jedermann* marks the beginning of the Salzburg Festival.

1938 German troops march into Austria and Salzburg becomes a Reichsgau.

1944–5 Salzburg is heavily bombed. In May 1945 American troops arrive.

1955 The Austrian state treaty and the proclamation of the Second Republic is signed. The country's neutrality is written into the constitution and the forces of occupation leave Austria.

1967 The first Easter Festival, founded by Herbert von Karajan, takes place.

1997 Salzburg's Old Town becomes a UNESCO world cultural heritage site.

2004 Salzburg's first female provincial governor is elected. The Modern Art Museum opens on the Mönchsberg.

2005 The 25th anniversary of the Alternative Nobel Prize is held in Salzburg.

2006 The 250th year anniversary of Mozart's birth.

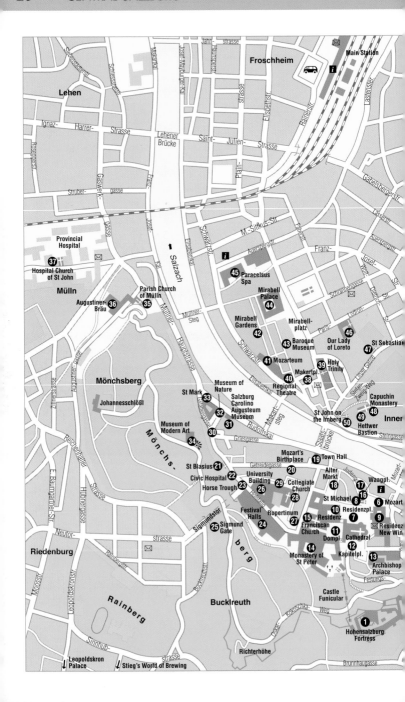

**ROUTES 1-6
SALZBURG**

0   300 m
0   300 yards

Schallmoos

Kapuzinerberg

Max Reinhardt
Research
Institute
(Arenberg Palace)

Salzach

emseehof
St Cajetan
④

nnberg
edictine
nvent
②

③
St Erhard
im Nonntal

Ibrunn Palace   Southern Bus Terminal

*Preceding pages: view from
Museum of Modern Art
Below: the city's western fringes
Bottom: shopping on the
Getreidegasse*

Map
on pages
20–21

Fortress Exhibitions
After a conducted tour of the fortress (every 40 mins) visit the **Rainer Museum** which recalls the Imperial and Royal Regiment of Archduke Rainer and the **Hohensalzburg Fortress Museum** containing a collection of artistic and cultural exhibits. The interesting **Marionette Museum**, in the cellars of the fortress, displays historical puppets from the Salzburg Marionette Theatre and is always a hit with children.

Ascending the Mönchsberg

1: The Fortress and Environs

Hohensalzburg Fortress – Nonnberg Benedictine Convent – St Erhard im Nonntal – Church of St Cajetan – Chiemseehof

★★★ **Hohensalzburg Fortress ❶** (open May– Sept 9am–9pm, Oct–April 9am–5pm) dominates the city's countenance like a crown of stone. Even if you have no time for an official conducted tour, you should still find time to stand on the vast Kuenburg Bastion and gaze down on the streets and houses. The fortress itself is well worth a few hours' attention if you have the time, as it is one of the largest and best-preserved fortresses in Europe. You can catch a funicular train up to the fortress at the end of the Festungsgasse. Alternatively, if you are feeling more energetic you can make your way up on foot (there is a staircase near the valley station). This will give you an opportunity to appreciate the precipitous nature of the rock (545–119 m/1,790–390 ft above the city) and the impregnability of the entire complex.

A citadel has stood on this rock since the time of the Romans. Work on the defensive complex that stands today was initiated by Archbishop Gebhard (1060–88), after he had taken the pope's side against the emperor in the Investiture Dispute. The fortress was built because Gebhard needed a means of defence against attacks by the troops of those who had remained faithful to the emperor.

THE FORTIFICATIONS

The fortress's present appearance is largely the result of building activity under Leonhard von Keutschach (1495–1519). Since the archbishops were not only churchmen but also powerful temporal rulers, they frequently needed the fortress as protection against forces from outside and revolts within their own territories. Repeatedly, the experience gained from these trials of strength was translated into continuous extensions and building projects. The original purpose of the various buildings is explained on wall plaques.

POINTS OF INTEREST

In the outer fortress courtyard stands a lime tree, which is several hundred years old, and the Fortress Well (1539). On the exterior wall of the Church of St George (1501–2) is an imposing marble memorial dedicated to Leonhard von Keutschach (1515).

The fortress interior can be visited as part of a conducted tour or you can make your own way round. The princely apartments and banqueting halls on the upper floor are some of the most beautiful Late Gothic secular interiors in the whole of Europe. Of particular interest are the Golden Hall, with magnificent wood panelling and carvings, and the Golden Room, in which stands a brightly-coloured porcelain tiled stove (1501). One curious exhibit is the Salzburg Bull, one of the earliest remaining street organs (1502). The horn mechanism was linked to a barrel mechanism in the middle of the 16th century. Renovation work began in 2000 and the organ now roars in reply to the Glockenspiel once again.

Star Attraction
•Hohensalzburg
Fortress

Below and bottom:
Hohensalzburg Fortress

THE NONNBERG CONVENT

The ★ **Nonnberg Benedictine Convent** ❷ was founded in *c*700 by St Rupert, who appointed his niece, St Erentrudis, as the first abbess. It is the

Map on pages 20–21

Below: winged altar, Chapel of St John
Bottom: Hohensalzburg Fortress

oldest convent to exist without interruption in the German-speaking countries. For this reason, only the church and the Chapel of St John can be visited. The robed figures on the South Door of the church, built between 1497–9, represent Emperor Henry II (the founding patron of the Romanesque church), St Mary the Virgin (the church's patron saint), St Rupert and St Erentrudis. The tympanum and the lintel are relics of the Romanesque church which burned down in 1423, the ground-plan of which was maintained when rebuilding began in 1463. Some frescoes (*c*1140) survived in the nuns' choir. They are being renovated, but you can see them if you put 50c in the slot. You should, however, make a point of collecting the key to the Chapel of St John (1448–51) from the convent entrance. Its winged altar (1498) is thought to have been painted by an artist who worked in close cooperation with Veit Stoss.

NONNTAL

If you walk round the convent building and along the Nonnberggasse, you will eventually come to the quiet, Biedermeier-style Nonntaler Hauptstrasse. The Erhardplatz gives the impression of being a garden in front of the church of **St Erhard im Nonntal ❸**. It was built between 1685–9 by the architect Johann Caspar Zuccalli, who orig-

inally came from the Swiss canton of Grisons. In the centre of the domed central building, which is richly ornamented with stucco, stands a beautiful high altar painting by the artist Johann Michael Rottmayr (1692), which is well worth investigating.

Star Attraction
• Church of St Cajetan

THE CHURCH OF ST CAJETAN

Building commenced at the same time on the ★★ **Church of St Cajetan** ❹ on the Kajetanplatz. Again, the architect in charge was Johann Caspar Zuccali. In this case, however, the work on the church itself and the wings of the priests' seminary was even more complicated and took considerably longer to complete.

The church was dedicated in 1700 but the interior was not completed until after 1730. The **interior** achieves its characteristic effect by means of the oval plan of the dome and the main body of the church, as well as the subtle stucco decoration and colour scheme.

The portrait of the Holy Family on the left side-altar is by Johann Michael Rottmayr (1708); all other altar paintings and the ceiling fresco (1728) were the work of Paul Troger. To the left of the main body of the church lies the Holy Staircase, built to a design based on the Scala Santa in Rome. It can be reached through the left-hand entrance door or, from the inside, via two chapels to the left of the main entrance.

KAIGASSE

The long rows of houses bordering the Kaigasse still recall their earlier history as the residence of former priests. The **Chiemseehof** ❺, Chiemseegasse 8, was from the beginning of the 14th century the residence of the bishops of Chiemsee in neighbouring Bavaria. The present appearance of the Chiemseehof is the result of extensive reconstruction during the late 17th century. It is unfortunately not possible to tour the building today as it now houses local government offices.

Johann Michael Rottmayer (1654–1730)
A renowned Baroque artist, born in Laufen, Salzburg Province, whose style was influenced by the Venetian art of painting in the 16th century. His specialty was ceiling frescos – he designed and executed most of the ceiling frescoes in the Salzburg Residenz and also in the Viennese Winter Riding School. He designed the altar in the University Church, Salzburg, and the original painting *The Apoteosis of St Charles Borromeo* (the intercessor for people stricken with the plague) which can be viewed in the Residenz Gallery.

Church of St Cajetan

Map on pages 20–21

2: A Melodic Meander

Mozartplatz – Residenzplatz – Cathedral – Kapitelplatz – Archbishop's Palace – Monastery of St Peter – Franciscan Church

The ★ **Mozart statue** on the **Mozartplatz ❻** was unveiled in 1842. The work of Ludwig Michael von Schwanthaler, it portrays the composer in a flowing cloak filled with inspiration, he is about to ascend Mount Parnassus, the home of the Muses.

Residenzplatz

Instead of climbing mountains whilst rapt in such lofty emotion, however, it is far more likely that the real Mozart would have headed for the Café Glockenspiel, which marks the way to the spacious ★★★ **Residenzplatz ❼**. The square represents the very heart of the princely baroque capital built with such enthusiasm by Archbishop Wolf Dietrich von Raitenau around 1600. Large numbers of medieval houses were demolished to make way for this magnificent square, whose fine focal point – an early baroque Renaissance-style **fountain** – was added in 1661. Every day the four aquatic horses spurting water can observe their living four-legged counterparts harnessed to the city's picturesque means of transport, the *fiakers*.

> **Is this Mozart?**
> The Mozart statue was erected to commemorate the 50th anniversary of Mozart's death. However, since the beginning the statue has caused a lot of controversy. Its erection was delayed by a year as, during on-site preparations, the remains of Roman mosaic tiles were found. On the 51st anniversary, the commemoration took place. Mozart's son performed; however, he only played a few of his father's works and then continued to perform some of his own compositions, before being dismissed from the stage. The statue itself it is not in Mozart's likeness – the composer died young. There is also an added discrepancy as he is holding a pencil – pencils were not invented until 20 or 30 years after his death; Mozart would have used a quill for composition.

Notable Buildings

The Residenzplatz is framed by a number of notable buildings. The **Church of St Michael ❽** was mentioned for the first time in 800 as the Palatinate Chapel. Its present form developed between 1767–76. To the east stands the **Residenz New Wing ❾**. Archbishop Wolf Dietrich began the construction of this section of his palace, originally consisting of four wings, in 1588, in order to provide appropriate accommodation for his guests. The modest facade is deceptive: inside, there are magnificent apartments with elaborately decorated ceilings. The heavy early baroque stucco work was the first example of its kind north of the Alps. Since the rooms are used

Priceless work fills the Residenz

today by the provincial government for receptions, the public may visit them only at certain times. Wolf Dietrich's successors extended his original building. The most original addition is the ★ **Glockenspiel** (closed weekends Nov–March), a musical instrument bought in Antwerp in 1695 by prince-bishop Johann Ernst von Thun. At 7am, 11am and 6pm daily, 35 bells play tunes including melodies by Haydn and Mozart.

Below: entering the Residenz
Bottom: imposing fountain on Residenzplatz

THE WEST SIDE

The west side of the Residenzplatz is occupied by the ★ **Residenz** ❿ (gallery closed Wed Jan–Feb, Mon March–Dec), whose origins stretch back as far as 1110, when the archbishop, who no longer held the office of Abbot of St Peter's, built himself the first Bishop's Palace. The Residenz's present-day appearance is the result of extensions and rebuilding begun by Archbishop Wolf Dietrich von Raitenau before 1600, but not completed until the late 18th century. The complex encloses three courtyards. The marble portal on the Residenzplatz leads into the main courtyard, whose interesting design should be noted. Passing through the triple-arched portico adorned with a Fountain of Hercules, take the staircase on the left which leads up to the sumptuous reception rooms. The priceless decorations adorning the audience rooms and the private apart-

Map on pages 20–21

Below: facade of the Cathedral
Bottom: Domplatz

ments of the archbishops are by a succession of famous artists, including Johann Michael Rottmayr, Martino Altomonte, Johann Lukas von Hildebrandt and Antonio Beduzzi. On the third floor is the Residenz Gallery, where European paintings from the 16th–19th century are displayed. The Salzburg Carolino Augusteum Museum *(see page 35)* is due to move here from its current location in 2006.

THE CATHEDRAL

Originally, Archbishop Wolf Dietrich also wanted to have the facade of the ★★ **Cathedral** realigned to give on to the Residenzplatz after the original building had burned down in a fire in 1598. However, his successor, Marcus Sitticus, cancelled this proposal when he commissioned his court architect, Santino Solari, to go ahead with the rebuilding. The alignment of the church remained as it had been when it was first built in 1181. The original cathedral on this spot had been built in 767–74 by St Virgil. The foundation stone of the new building was laid in 1614, and the cathedral was rededicated in 1628.

Solari found his inspiration in the Italian tradition of church architecture. On the west side of the cathedral he erected the first post-medieval facade with twin towers north of the Alps; it became the model for many churches in the South German region. The porch is entered through three arched openings flanked by statues of Saints Virgil and Rupert (outside) and Saints Peter and Paul (inside). The broad, barrel-vaulted nave is flanked by rows of chapels and leads into the choir and transepts, which are flooded with light and arranged in a clover-leaf formation around the domed crossing. The ceiling paintings on the inside of the dome had to be reconstructed following severe damage during World War II. The cathedral interior dates largely from the 17th century; of the old cathedral, only the font (1321) supported by four lions (12th-century) remains. The entrance to the worthwhile ★ **Cathedral Museum** is situated in the porch and there is also a museum dedicated to the cathedral's excavations.

DOMPLATZ AND KAPITELPLATZ

The West Front of the cathedral is framed by the courtyard-like ★**Domplatz** ⓫. The square is the setting for the annual performances of *Jedermann* (Everyman), which take place under the stony surveillance of Saints Virgil and Rupert (with bishop's crook) and Saints Peter (with keys) and Paul (with sword).

The Column of the Virgin Mary was created by the Hagenauer brothers in 1766–71. It must have been part of the original plan for the cathedral facade, for if you stand under the arcades to the west of the square and look across at the statue of the Virgin, you will observe that the two angels sitting on the gable above the central window on the cathedral facade appear to be holding the crown exactly above the head of the Madonna.

The spacious layout of the **Kapitelplatz** ⓬ also formed part of Archbishop Wolf Dietrich's grandiose plan. The horses' drinking trough adorned by Poseidon on a sea-horse was designed in 1732 on the instructions of Archbishop Leopold Anton Firmian. To the left lies the **Archbishop's Palace** ⓭. The regal buildings were the headquarters of the Cathedral Chapter until 1864; they housed the priests' college and their apartments (Kanonikalhöfe). After this date they served as the private residence of the archbishops.

Star Attraction
• **The Cathedral**

St Virgil
One of the early bishops of Salzburg, St Virgil was an Irish missionary known in Ireland as Ferghal, who ruled Salzburg in the mid 8th century. He was responsible for building the first cathedral; however, as a large wooden structure its fate was a fiery demise, as was the original St Peter's. In recognition of his work, he is honoured with a statue in the main entrance of the cathedral.

Stalls on Kapitelplatz

Map on pages 20–21

St Peter's Cemetery

The cemetery behind St Peter's Monastery is the elegant, even romantic, resting place of Salzburg's noblest families. It is located at the base of the Mönchsberg and is the oldest cemetery in Salzburg still in use. The present layout of the churchyard dates from 1627 and, on first impression, the burial plots seem haphazardly laid out. Most of the graves have markers which have an enamel centrepiece painted with rich colours. Many of these have a lamp dangling from the post supporting the elaborate design. In the centre of the graveyard lies St Margaret's Chapel which holds the remains of Mozart's sister, Nannerl, and the famous musician Michael Haydn. Also of note are the catacombs that are built into the mountain above the cemetery. They are believed to be some of the earliest Christian prayer sites in Europe.

St Peter's Cemetery

MONASTERY OF ST PETER

In the west is the extensive complex of the ★★ **Monastery of St Peter** ⑭. The oldest section can be seen if you cross the peaceful **cemetery**, tucked away at the foot of the Mönchsberg. The **catacombs** were reputedly carved into the rock wall in ancient times. The monastery was reorganised by St Rupert in about 696 and experienced its first Golden Age under St Virgil. The buildings reveal traces of every architectural epoch since then. A remarkable example of this mixture of styles can be seen in the Romanesque tower of the Monastery Church, which is surmounted by a baroque cupola. Even the porch demonstrates that the church is basically High Romanesque. The late-baroque transformation was carried out under Abbot Beda Seeauer (1753–86). Almost all the altar paintings are by Martin Johann Schmidt (Schmidt of Krems), and exhibit his characteristic style with its contrasts of light and dark. The cloisters to the north of the church are a mixture of Romanesque and Gothic styles and form part of the monastery; unfortunately they are closed to the public. To the right of the church entrance lies the **Peterskeller**, which has been a wine tavern since 803.

FRANCISCAN CHURCH

Crossing the Stiftshof with its St Peter's Fountain you will arrive in front of the ★ **Franciscan Church** ⑮, which should be entered via the West Door situated in the Sigmund-Haffner-Gasse. Walk through the dark nave of the earlier Romanesque building, dedicated in 1223, up to the late-Gothic hall choir, which is flooded with light. The latter was begun in 1422 by the famous architect Hans von Burghausen and completed in 1460 by Stephan Krumenauer. In the middle is the high altar designed by Johann Bernhard Fischer von Erlach in 1709, which provides a worthy setting for a late-Gothic statue of the Virgin Mary (1485–98) by Michael Pacher. Above the nave is the oratory, which looks like the facade of a house. It was commissioned by Wolf Dietrich von Raitenau in 1606 to provide a link between the church and the Residenz.

3: Fountains, Horses and Poetry

**Waagplatz – Alter Markt – Mozart's Birthplace
– Church of St Blasius – Horse Trough – Festival
Halls – University – Collegiate Church**

Map
on pages
20–21

During the Middle Ages, the **Waagplatz** 🛈 was
the city's main square, a lively area that had a market, granary, municipal courts, a town hall and many
other attractions. The Romanische Keller (No. 4,
now an exhibition gallery) is all that remains of
the 12th-century imperial palace. The poet Georg
Trakl was born at No. 1a (Memorial Museum and
Research Centre; tours Mon–Fri 11am and 2pm).
Some of his lyric poems are engraved on marble
plaques which can be seen throughout the city.

Star Attraction
•**St Peter's Monastery**

ALTER MARKT

The Jewish population of Salzburg lived in the narrow **Judengasse** 🛈 until 1498, when they were
expelled by Archbishop Leonhard von Keutschach.
The ★ **Alter Markt** 🛈 owes its cheerful countenance to the **pastel-coloured facades** of the surrounding houses with their delicate stucco
decorations. In the centre stands a fountain,
bedecked with flowers, an ornamental wrought-
iron railing (1583) and a statue of St Florian (1734).
A curiosity is the smallest house in the city (10a).
You can still buy medicines in the ★ **Hofapotheke**

Below: the chemist's shop
Bottom: shoppers stroll

Map on pages 20–21

Johann Fischer von Erlach (1656–1723) One of the most prolific architects of the Baroque period, von Erlach spent the years 1693–9 in Salzburg where he renovated almost every church including the Collegiate Church, St Mark's Church, the Church of the Holy Trinity and the Hospital Church of St John.

Mozart's birthplace on the Getreidegasse

opposite, a chemist's shop which once served the court of the prince-bishops. The **Café Tomaselli** has stood here since 1705.

TOWN HALL

The **Town Hall ⓲**, topped by a bell-tower, was built in 1407 and reconstructed between 1616–8. The facade, (which dates from 1772) is unassuming in appearance, reflecting the fact that the town was still under the sway of the archbishops at that time, who kept a watchful eye to ensure that no signs of budding civic consciousness were given expression in flights of architectural magnificence. It was only in the design of the passageways between the streets – known as *Durchhäuser* – that the ordinary citizen was allowed more freedom. These passageways lead off the **Getreidegasse**, one of the city's oldest streets. The first mention of such a passageway occurs in 1363 and refers to the Treasure Passageway (No. 3), which has a pretty inner courtyard. A forest of ancient or ancient-looking shop signs indicates that you are in Salzburg's main shopping street. The Getreidegasse is, however, also a pilgrimage trail for Mozart fans. Here you will find ★★★ **Mozart's Birthplace ⓴**. Wolfgang Amadeus Mozart was born here on 27 January 1756, and it was here that he and his family lived until they moved to the house on the Makartplatz *(see page 37)* in 1773. The Mozart family apartment on the third floor and the rooms on the second floor have been transformed into a museum.

CHURCH OF ST BLASIUS

The ★ **Church of St Blasius** (Hospital Church) ㉑, one of the oldest Gothic hall churches in existence (1330–50), has a gallery extending past the middle of the church, on which the patients were once able to take part in the service. One of the church's most remarkable treasures is the ★ **tabernacle** containing the Sacrament, dating from 1480. Designed in the form of a church, it can be seen to the left of the high altar. Directly adjacent on the south side is the former **Civic Hospital ㉒**, which was founded in 1327. The lovely three-storey arcaded courtyard was built during the Renaissance. Today the hospital building houses the Toy Museum.

HORSE TROUGH AND FESTIVAL HALLS

The ★★ **Horse Trough** ❷ of the royal stables was originally designed in 1695 by Johann Bernhard Fischer von Erlach. The sculpture group portraying the horse-tamer (by Bernhard Michael Mandl) originally looked across at the facade of the former royal stables, also designed by Fischer von Erlach. In 1732 the group was turned through 90° as part of a rearrangement of the horse trough.

We now come to the ★ **Festival Halls** ❷. Until the end of the 17th century, the stables (erected in 1607 under Wolf Dietrich von Raitenau) included a winter and a summer riding school. In 1925, Eduard Hütter converted the military riding school (a 19th-century addition) into a Festival Hall. The latter was enlarged in 1926 and again between 1936–7 by Clemens Holzmeister. However, the increasing popularity of the Salzburg Festival meant that an even larger theatre was needed. Between 1956–60, the Large Festival Hall was built, designed by Holzmeister. It retained the stable facade and added a 60-m (197-ft) high stage, partly built into the Mönchsberg. The old hall became the Small Festival Hall. The Summer Rid-

Below: Toy Museum
Bottom: the Festival Halls

Map on pages 20–21

ing School, also built into the mountain face, with its arcades cut into the rock according to a design by Fischer von Erlach, was transformed into an open-air stage as early as 1926. It was redesigned and roofed in 1968–9 by Clemens Holzmeister. Today the three auditoriums can accommodate some 5,000 spectators. The Winter Riding School, with a spectacular ceiling fresco by Johann Michael Rottmayr and Christoph Lederwasch (1690), serves as a foyer during the intervals in performances.

Clemens Holzmeister (1886–1983)
Holzmeister was a famous Austrian architect who was an influential creator of monuments and religious structures. He was also known as a set designer. He was responsible for the renovation of the Festival Halls in 1926 and 1936–38 as well as the designs for the new festival hall in 1955–60. He is buried in St Peter's Cemetery.

RUPERTINUM

The **Sigmund Gate** ㉕ was cut through the narrowest section of the Mönchsberg between 1764–7. The side of the Hofstallgasse opposite the Festival Halls is bordered by the old **University Building** ㉖, which was built between 1618–55. The long, drawn-out complex opens up on Max-Reinhard-Platz towards the Wilhelm Furtwängler Park, a little oasis of green whose entrance is guarded by the **Wild Man on the Fish** Fountain (1620). The remaining side of the square is delineated by the **Rupertinum** ㉗. The building was erected in 1630 and renovated between 1979–82. Today, it houses an important art collection of 20th-century art works. The main collection was moved to the new Museum on the Mönchsberg in 2004.

The Rupertinum

COLLEGIATE CHURCH

The university complex is completed by the ★★ **Collegiate Church** ㉘, one of Johann Bernhard Fischer von Erlach's greatest masterpieces. The facade, with its protruding arched central section and the flanking towers, became the model for many baroque buildings in the South German area. The interior is surprisingly high and has an unusually rigid structural form. The far side of the choir forms a stark contrast as a host of angels on stucco clouds hover around a Madonna wreathed in rays of light.

The **University Square** ㉙ presents a colourful picture when the daily ★ **vegetable market** is held and the farmers and traders set up their stalls.

4: Up the Mönchsberg

**Gstättengasse – St Mark's Church – Parish
Church of Mülln**

The **Gstättengasse ❸**, bordered by tall townhouses leaning into the rocky face of the Mönchsberg, leads through the Gstättentor, a gateway
surmounted by a house, passing the oldest baker's
shop in Salzburg (1429, No. 4) before reaching
Anton-Neumayr-Platz, which adjoins the
Museum Square. This is the location of the
★ **Salzburg Carolino Augusteum Museum ❸**.
In the main building (No. 1) are interesting items
relating to the history of the town as well as its art
and culture *(see pages 101–109)*. In 2006, the
museum moves to the Residenz building *(see
page 28)* The nearby ★ **Museum of Nature ❸**
is more than just a natural history museum; it also
offers an unusual 'World of Experiences' with
a space hall, aquarium, reptile zoo and much
more. It is housed in the premises formerly occupied by the Ursuline Convent, founded in 1695.
The site became available in 1957 when the nuns
moved to a new location on the edge of town.

The former Ursuline Chapel is now known as
St Mark's Church ❸. Its wedge-shaped ground-
plan was a challenge for the architect, Johann
Bernhard Fischer von Erlach. It was built between
1699–1705 after a massive mountainside on 16

Map
on pages
20–21

Star Attraction
• **Collegiate Church**

Below: Gstättengasse
Bottom: Museum of Nature

Map
on pages
20–21

*Below : the restaurant in the
Museum of Modern Art
Bottom: outside the
Museum of Modern Art*

July 1669 had destroyed the previous building and killed 220 people. Since that date, 'mountain cleaners' tap the city's mountains every year to check whether there are any loose stones.

You can reach the top of the **Mönchsberg** by taking the new lift (entrance at Gstättengasse 13). At the top, is the magnificent ★ ★ **Museum of Modern Art ㉞**. Opened in 2004, the museum is dedicated to contemporary painting sculpture, graphic design and contains the Austrian Gallery of Photography. In front of the museum you can enjoy one of the best panoramas of the town.

MÜLLN

The **Parish Church of Mülln ㉟** provides a fitting conclusion to the overall picture of the Old Town. It is a late-Gothic buttressed church (1439–53) with an interior dating from 1738. The stucco work is characterised by delicate baroque foliage and ribbons. The church once belonged to a monastery of Augustine hermit monks. A staircase to the left leads down into the spacious vaulted cellars of the **Augustiner-Bräu ㊱**, a brewery tavern with a beer garden. In the summer this is a popular haunt for both visitors and locals.

Within the grounds of the Regional Hospital lies the **Hospital Church of St John ㊲** (1704), also the work of J B Fischer von Erlach.

5: The Mozart Trail

Makartplatz – Church of the Holy Trinity – Mozarteum – Mirabell Palace – Church of Our Lady of Loreto – Church of St Sebastian

Map on pages 20–21

Star Attraction
• **Museum of Modern Art**

The ★ **Makartplatz** ❸ is framed not only by 18th/19th-century buildings, but also unfortunately by a postwar architectural monstrosity. **Mozart's House (No. 9)** was badly damaged during World War II and only about one-third of the building in which Leopold Mozart and his family had rented a flat between 1773–87 survived. The Mozarteum International Foundation reconstructed and enlarged the house in 1996, enabling the ★ **Memorial Museum** to be extended. As well as recounting the history of the great composer, the museum also houses a collection of old musical instruments.

The **Church of the Holy Trinity** ❸ was built between 1694–1702 by J B Fischer von Erlach and dominates the square. Its powerful central section, flanked by the facades of the former priest's house.

Mozart Year 2006

In 2006 Salzburg will be playing a major role in the 250th birthday celebrations of the man who is considered by many to be the greatest musical genius of all times. Among the planned festivities will be the performance of all his operas and musical theatre works during the Salzburg Festival. The small festival hall, now renamed the 'House for Mozart', will reopen in July 2006 having been completely rebuilt. There will be an exhibition in the new Salzburg Museum on Mozartplatz. 'Viva Mozart' will run for the entire year and will encompass virtual reality displays.

THEATRES

The **Landestheater** ❹ was built between 1892–3 and was reconstructed in 1938. Behind is the Studio Theatre, the Puppet Theatre and the ★ **Mozarteum** ❹, the headquarters of a foundation dedicated to Mozart's music, as well as departments of the College of Music and Dramatic Arts. During July and August conducted tours are available through the concert and college building, which were built between 1910–14 in neoclassical, neo-baroque and Secessionist style. Also in the tour are visits to Mozart's apartment and the Magic Flute Cottage, a summer house in which Mozart is supposed to have composed his famous last opera. It originally stood in Vienna near the Theater an der Wien, but was donated to the city of Salzburg in 1873.

Memorial Museum

MIRABELL GARDENS

The garden of the Mozarteum adjoins the ★★ **Mirabell Gardens** ❹, whose geometrical layout is decorated with sculptures based on clas-

Map on pages 20–21

Paracelsus Spa

The northern boundary of the Mirabell Gardens is set by the modern Congress House and the modern **Paracelsus Spa**, which is open to the public. Since 1968, Salzburg has been an officially recognised spa town because of the healing agents of mud, brine and mineral water.

sical mythology. It has remained virtually unchanged since it was redesigned in 1730 by Franz Anton Danreiter. The original scheme (1689) was attributed to J B Fischer von Erlach. On the west side of the parterre is an open-air theatre with trimmed hedges marking the wings and entrances, the **Dwarf Garden** with an amusing collection of marble dwarfs (c1715) and the aviary (now a museum pavilion).

The pretty Rose Garden in front of the castle is framed by a balustrade. On the east side lie the Orangery (which includes a Palm House) and a charming **Baroque Museum** ㊸ (open Sun 10am–1pm, closed Mon) containing an important collection of oil sketches, drawings and sculpture models.

THE PALACE

★ **Mirabell Palace** ㊹ (open Mon, Wed, Thurs 8am–4pm, Tues, Fri 1–4pm, Sat 8am–1pm) was built in 1606 by Archbishop Wolf Dietrich von Raitenau as a country house for his mistress Salome Alt and their 15 children. Its name in those days was *Altenau*; the building was rechristened on the orders of Marcus Sitticus in an attempt to erase the memory of his predecessor's unseemly relationship. Under Archbishop Franz Anton Harrach the building was reconstructed between

Blooms in the palace gardens

1721–27 in accordance with plans by Johann Lukas von Hildebrandt. Following the great fire of 1818 the palace was again reconstructed, but in a less extravagant manner. Today the palace houses the municipal administration and library, but it is still possible to imagine what it must have been like in more opulent times. Visitors drove in through the entrance in their carriages, crossing the courtyard to the vestibule of the garden wing with its delicate stucco ornaments. Here they descended and climbed the magnificent main staircase whose curving balustrade was adorned with acrobatic **cherubs** (the work of Georg Raphael Donner) accompanying the guests to the top of the stairs.

Arriving on the first floor they entered the ★ **Marble Hall**, richly adorned with stucco decorations. Formerly the dining room, today it is the setting for concerts.

THE CHURCH OF OUR LADY OF LORETO

The **Church of Our Lady of Loreto** ❹❻ and the adjoining convent were built for nuns who fled from Landshut in Bavaria in 1633 before the advancing Swedish troops during the Thirty Years' War.

The ★ **Church of St Sebastian** ❹❼ was built in 1749–53, replacing a building dating from the early 16th century; the cemetery was also part of the earlier complex. Wolf Dietrich had the latter transformed into an Italian *Campo Santo*, the only one of its kind north of the Alps. Almost exactly square in shape, it is surrounded by four arcades. In the centre he placed his own mausoleum, built between 1597–1603, with space all round for the wealthy citizens of Salzburg to rest in eternal peace. The **Chapel of St Gabriel** behind the church is remarkable for the unusual manner in which the interior walls are clad with tiny coloured ceramic tiles. These contrast dramatically with the brilliant white stucco, creating an atmosphere of tranquillity. Amongst the gravestones you will find a number of familiar names: Mozart's wife Constanze, his father Leopold and the famous doctor Paracelsus.

Star Attraction
• **Mirabell Gardens and Palace**

Below: Mirabell Gardens
Bottom: St Sebastian's Church

6: Palaces, Gardens, then Beer

Capuchin Monastery – Hettwer Bastion – Leopoldskron Palace – Stiegl's World of Brewing – Hellbrunn Palace

Map on pages 20–21

St John on the Imberg

A short, steep path named after Stefan Zweig begins beside the gateway of the house at No. 14 Linzergasse. The writer lived in the Paschinger Mansion (Kapuzinerberg 5) between 1919–38. Passing the Stations of the Cross, chapels and a crucifixion group (1780) you will arrive at the **Capuchin Monastery ㊽**. The monastery was commissioned by Wolf Dietrich for monks whom he had summoned to Salzburg and was built between 1599–1602 on the ruins of an old fortification complex. The **Hettwer Bastion ㊾** affords a ★ **panorama** of the city which is seen at its best in the early morning or evening light. The Kapuzinerberg provides a pleasant setting for long walks.

STEINGASSE

If you descend via the Imbergstiege, take a look at the little church of **St John on the Imberg ㊿** (1681), which seems to cling to the face of the mountain. The narrow ★ **Steingasse** snakes along the Kapuzinerberg. Many of the tall houses here date from the Middle Ages. The road eventually becomes the Arenbergstrasse and leads to **Arenberg Palace**, built in the Biedermeier style. Between 1912–22 it was the home of the Austrian dramatist and novelist Hermann Bahr (1863–1934). Since 1968 it has been the home of the Max Reinhardt Research Institute. The institute's scientific work on the theatrical world are on display at the Festival Halls *(see page 33)*.

LEOPOLDSKRON

★★ **Leopoldskron Palace**, to the south of the town centre *(see map on page 43)*, is the loveliest example of secular baroque architecture in the city. Surrounded by parkland, it enjoys an idyllic situation beside its own artificial lake. Unfortunately the interior is not open to the public and no guided

Stefan Zweig (1881–1942)

An influential Austrian author of Jewish origin, Zweig described himself as an 'accidental Jew'. He spent the years between the two world wars in Salzburg. This was his most prolific and productive period. In 1934 he fled Austria, first to England and eventually to South America. He and his wife committed suicide together as they despaired of the future of Europe.

tours are available. Work on the palace itself began in 1736 on the orders of prince-bishop Leopold Anton Firmian. In 1918 the castle was purchased by Max Reinhardt, who turned it into a rendezvous for artists and intellectuals. After World War II it was acquired by Harvard University, which runs its Salzburg Seminar in American Studies here.

★**Stiegl's World of Brewing** (open Thurs–Sun 10am–4pm) to the west of the town centre is the largest private brewery in Austria, and its extensive museum traces the brewing process from start to finish.

HELLBRUNN PALACE

★★ **Hellbrunn Palace** was built as a summer residence by prince-bishop Marcus Sitticus. It lies beyond the city limits in the countryside, but can quickly be reached from the town centre *(see map on page 43)*. Bordered by 300-year-old trees, the traffic-free Hellbrunner Allee runs from Freisal Palace in the Nonntal past a number of other palaces and mansions to Hellbrunn. The layout and design of the palace itself follow the lines of a typical Italian *villa suburbana*. It was probably built between 1613–5 under the supervision of the architect in charge of the reconstruction of the cathedral, Santino Solari. The interior is no longer complete, but the frescoes in the banqueting hall and the

Star Attraction
• **Hellbrunn Palace**

Below: Hellbrunn Palace
Bottom: Kapuzinerberg

Map
on page
43

Markus Sittikus

The nephew of the famed Archbishop Wolf Dietrich, Markus Sittikus was the archbishop of Salzburg for seven years in the 17th century. During this time he maintained the architectural movement begun by his uncle and finished the cathedral as we know it today, built many other churches and the city gates. Hellbrunn Palace was also built by him and where he added his own personal touches. He also had a great love of music and theatre and he bought the first performance of Italian opera to Germanic soil in the outdoor theatre in Hellbrunn.

adjoining **music room** in the octagonal pavilion still provide first-class examples of the Mannerist style: with views of a city in the background, the *trompe-l'oeil* painting shows imaginary scenes of buildings with aristocrats strolling among them.

HELLBRUNN GARDENS

The palace's main attractions are the ★ **Surprise Fountains** in the garden. The bishop had the idea of having them built following a lengthy stay in Rome; here, however, he carried the surprise element to extremes. Unexpectedly, water fountains would suddenly gush forth from the stone seats and soak the guests sitting at the table in the Roman theatre – except for the bishop himself, who was vastly amused at the joke. Visitors should also be prepared for surprises in the various grottoes, which are arranged according to mythological themes. Nowadays the guides are equally unconcerned about water damage to the expensive cameras carried by visitors – so beware! Hydraulic power is also used to drive a number of smaller machines and a large **mechanical theatre** with an organ which runs on water power.

Hellbrunn Palace and Gardens

ALSO OF INTEREST

On Hellbrunn Mountain you will also find the Monatsschlössl (1615), now a Folklore Museum, the **Stone Theatre** (probably the oldest open-air stage in the German-speaking region) and the **Zoo**. Situated just past Hellbrunn Palace, the zoo has an impressive collection of birds and mammals from around the world. Some of the highlights include the tigers and rhinos. The use of semi-open pens means that visitors can get close to the animals. Some of the birds, such as the vultures or flamingos can be seen either around the peak of the Untersberg, or in Leopoldskron farm ponds. Feeding times are especially interesting and in the summer, the zoo is sometimes open at night.

Every year, on the first and second weekend in August, the Hellbrunn Festival is held featuring operas, plays and concerts.

Sights in the Vicinity

Map below

★ **Klessheim Palace** was originally planned by Archbishop Johann Ernst Thun as a pheasant-breeding farm, but it eventually became a summer palace. It was built between 1700–9 under the architect J B Fischer von Erlach. By 1732 the interior and the vast approach ramp had been completed; standing photogenically on each side of the latter are four stags with stars in their antlers. In the former pheasant run (today a golf course) stands the so-called Hoyos-Stöckl, a garden pavilion designed by Fischer von Erlach with a petal-shaped floor-plan. Hitler chose the palace as his residence when he was staying in Salzburg. The palace also houses the Salzburg Casino. The interior of the palace can be seen only during the major exhibitions held here from time to time.

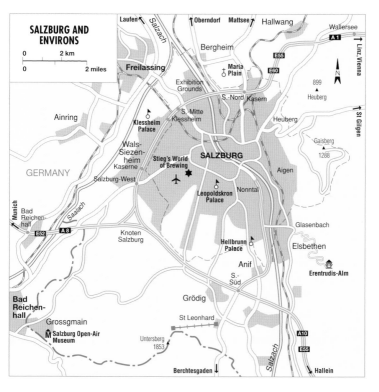

Map on page 43

Hangar-7
Salzburg's most spectacular hangar near Salzburg airport not only houses the Flying Bulls collection of vintage aircraft, but also holds art exhibitions. It is a unique combination of architectural elegance, engineering excellence and interesting works of art.

Maria Plain

Anif, neo-Gothic moated castle

Day trips from town

★★ **Maria Plain** (1671–4), situated 5 km/3 miles north of Salzburg, is a pilgrimage church built by court architect Giovanni Antonio Dario from a commission by Archbishop Max Gandolf Kuenberg. Mozart's Coronation Mass is performed here every year on the Feast of the Assumption (15 August). You can pick up the footpath following the Stations of the Cross at the Plainbrücke (Lokalbahn train S1 o S11, then it's a 30-minute walk).

★ **Anif** (pop. 4,200; 6 km/4 miles south of Salzburg) is famous for its 16th-century reconstructed neo-Gothic moated castle (private property), which is surrounded by landscaped gardens. Herbert von Karajan, who lived here, is buried in the village cemetery.

Some 5 km (3 miles) further south, in St Leonhard, you can catch a cable car to the Geiereck on the **Untersberg** (1,853 m/6,078 ft). The plateau-shaped massif is shrouded in myth and at the top you can enjoy the view, rest in the mountain refuge or visit the Hochalm restaurant. Catch the No. 25 bus from Salzburg to the valley station.

At the western foot of the Untersberg lies the ★ **Salzburg Open-air Museum** (closed Mon) at Grossgmain, where 40 historic farm buildings from the Salzburg region have been reconstructed with meticulous care. Here, you can relive a vanished world of rural life and its culture.

1: Silent Night Trip

Salzburg – Mattsee – Michaelbeuern – Salzburg (80 km/50 miles)

Map on page 46–47

'If anyone had asked me in those days where Paradise was, I would have answered without hesitation: in Austria, 16 km (10 miles) east of Salzburg on the Imperial Road, right by the Wallersee,' reminisces the German dramatist Carl Zuckmayer in his autobiography *Als wär's ein Stück von mir* ('A Part of Myself'), looking back on the period he spent in Henndorf (1926–38). If you follow the proposed route you will be able to decide for yourself whether you agree with him. To reach the area, leave Salzburg on the B1 *(see map on pages 46–7)*. The Wiesmühl, Zuckmayer's house in **Henndorf am Wallersee**, is private property and can only be viewed from the outside. By way of compensation, however, you can enjoy the atmosphere in the historic dining-room of the Caspar-Moser-Bräu, where Zuckmayer was a frequent guest.

Star Attraction
• **Mattsee**

MATTSEE

After passing Neumarkt am Wallersee (campsite, 22 km/14 miles), leave the B1 towards Köstendorf (baroque Church of the Nativity of the Virgin Mary). Shortly before **Mattsee** (pop. 2,500; 33 km/21 miles), the road skirts round a section of the Buchberg (800 m/2,625 ft), with a view across the Flachgau. The village itself lies on a spit of land which separates the Mattsee (also Niedertrumer See) from the Obertrumer See. It is thought the monastery was founded by Duke Tassilo of Bavaria some time after 777. Until the mid 11th century it was a Benedictine monastery; it then became a collegiate abbey. The Romanesque-Gothic collegiate church acquired its present form when it was rebuilt in the baroque style around 1700. The monastery museum contains a number of exhibits from its golden age. Behind the monastery are the ruins of the castle of the former local lord; to the right is an open-air museum with a reconstructed Bavarian farmstead. *(Information: Tourist Office, Marketplatz 1, A-5163 Mattsee, tel: 06217-6080.)*

Mattsee

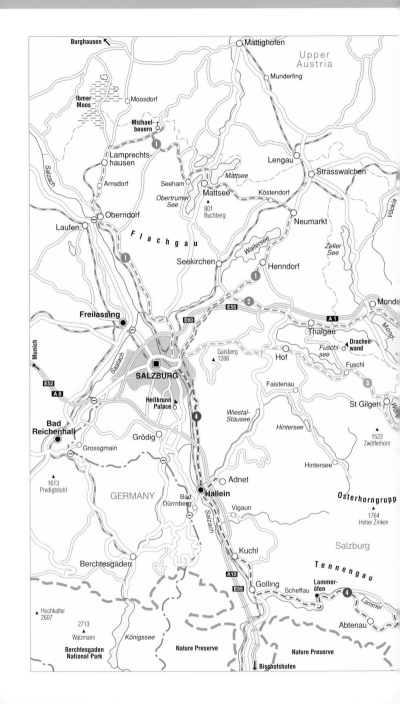

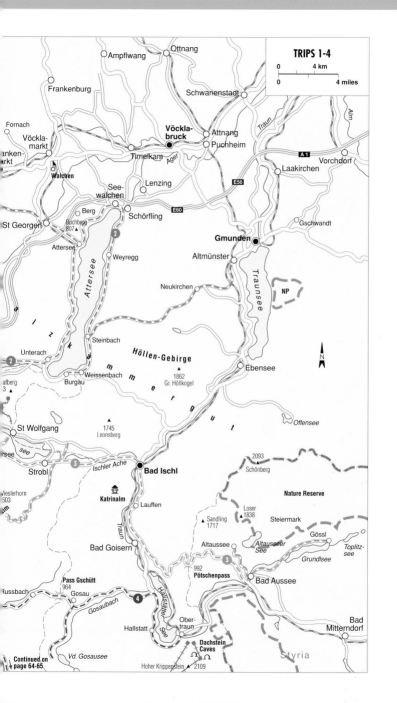

TRIPS 1-4

0   4 km
0   4 miles

Ottnang
Ampflwang
Frankenburg
Schwanenstadt
Fornach
Vöckla-
markt
anken-
arkt
Vöckla-
bruck
Attnang
Puchheim
Timelkam
Ager
Traun
Alm
A 1
Vorchdorf
Laakirchen
Walchen
E56
Seewalchen
Lenzing
E60
Berg
Schörfling
St Georgen
Buchberg
807
Attersee
Gmunden
Gschwandt
Weyregg
Altmünster
Attersee
Neukirchen
Traunsee
NP
Steinbach
Höllen-Gebirge
Unterach
Weissenbach
Burgau
1862
Gr. Höllkogel
Ebensee
afberg
3
1745
Leonsberg
Offensee
St Wolfgang
see
2093
Schönberg
Nature Reserve
Strobl
Ischler Ache
Bad Ischl
Vieslerhorn
603
m
Katrinalm
Lauffen
Loser
1838
Steiermark
Sandling
1717
Altaussee
Altausseer
See
Gössl
Toplitz-
see
Bad Goisern
Grundlsee
Traun
992
Pötschenpass
Bad Aussee
Pass Gschütt
964
Russbach
Gosau
Gosaubach
Hallstätter See
Bad
Mitterndorf
Hallstatt
Ober-
traun
Dachstein
Caves
Styria
Continued on
page 64-65
Vd. Gosause
Hoher Krippenstein
2109

Map
on pages
46–47

Silent Night

The first performance of the famous Christmas carol took place in the parish church of **Oberndorf** (pop. 4,800; 62 km/39 miles). On the site of the parish church of St Nicholas, which was demolished in 1900, there stands today the **Silent Night Memorial Chapel.** Adjacent to the chapel is an interesting local museum.

MICHAELBEUERN

Shortly before Seeham there is a twisting stretch of road leading to ★★**Michaelbeuern**, 45 km (30 miles) away. The **Benedictine abbey** here is thought to have been founded in the 8th century. The Chapter Room and lower storey of the refectory date from Romanesque times. The abbey room received its stucco decorations around 1720 and is adorned with ceiling and wall paintings which date from 1771. The beautiful two-storey library (1769–79) is relatively unadorned and contains 40,000 volumes. Outstanding among the 300 manuscripts is the famous Walther Bible (mid-12th-century), an important example of the Salzburg book illuminator's art.

The Gothic and baroque transformations of the Romanesque abbey church were largely removed during restoration (1938–50). Some sections, including the wooden ceiling, were reconstructed in Romanesque style. The most famous item in the abbey is the high altar (1691–2) with statues by Meinrad Guggenbichler and pictures by Johann Michael Rottmayr.

ARNSDORF AND OBERNDORF

Approaching the Bürmoos and the Waldmoos, which together with the Ibmer Moos in Upper Austria form the largest moorland region in the

Michaelbeuern Abbey

country, the industrial extraction of peat has denuded many areas.

Shortly before Lamprechtshausen you will reach the B156. The next two villages have gone down in history as the birthplaces of *Silent Night, Holy Night*. In **Arnsdorf** (57 km/36 miles), near the pilgrimage church of St Mary, a folklore museum has been created in the former school house in which the schoolmaster and organist Franz Xaver Gruber composed the famous Christmas carol.

Until 1816, Oberndorf was a suburb of Laufen, which lies in Bavaria on the opposite bank of the Salzach. The Folklore Museum, the **River Festival** – held each year in August – and the **Pirates' Battle** held every five years recall Oberndorf's importance for navigation on the Salzach. You can reach the pilgrimage church of St Mary by means of a Calvary stair and an avenue. The building is a small, playfully baroque edifice. Continuing along the B156 it is now only 18 km (10 miles) to Salzburg.

OBERNDORF – SILENT NIGHT MEMORIAL CHAPEL

Almost 200 years ago, in 1818, the first rendition of the famous carol, *Silent Night, Holy Night* was performed in **Oberndorf** in St Nikolaus Church. Created by Franz Xaver, a schoolmaster and organist, the carol has become one of the most well known and loved of the festive season. Unfortunately, the original St Nikolaus Church was demolished as Oberndorf was re-located due to the floods in the late 1800s.

The memorial chapel, which sits on the site of the original church, was consecrated in 1937 and every year at 5pm on 24 Dec, a memorial service takes place with thousands of people attending. The Museum of Local History next to the memorial chapel provides an in depth look into the lives and history of all those involved in the carol (Stille-Nacht-Platz 7, Oberndorf bei Salzburg, tel: 06272/4422, open daily 9am–4pm, closed in February).

Star Attraction
• Michaelbeuern

Silent Night stained glass window and Memorial Chapel

Map
on pages
46–47

*Below: Parish church of
St Michael
Bottom: Mondsee*

2: Call Of The Lakes

Salzburg – Mondsee – Attersee (55 km/34 miles)

The quickest way of reaching Mondsee from Salzburg is via the A1 motorway; for a more pleasant approach, however, take the B1, which leads through Thalgau (parish church of St Martin, 1747–9).

★★ **Mondsee** (pop. 3,000; 27 km/16 miles), lies on the northwest tip of the lake. The area was inhabited in Neolithic times, as remaining pile dwellings testify. The inhabitants were the representatives of the Mondsee culture (1900–1700 BC). With the foundation of the monastery – the third-oldest in Austria – by Duke Odilo II of Bavaria in 748, Mondsee grew to become the cultural centre of the Salzburg-Bavaria region. In 1791 the monastery was dissolved; a large number of treasures, including all the books, were taken to Linz and Vienna.

MONDSEE MONASTERY

The oldest parts of the monastery building, converted into a palace after the closure of the monastery, date from the late Gothic era (chapter house, cloister). The main section was built following a serious fire in 1774. The former monastery church is today the Parish Church of **St Michael**. Standing on the market square, it was built

between 1470–87 to replace a high-Romanesque building. The baroque facade was added in 1730, the towers were also extended and in 1774 the hipped roof was constructed. Underneath, however, remained the generously proportioned late-Gothic basilica (70 m/230 ft long, 33 m/108 ft wide and 29 m/95 ft high). The high altar dates from the Renaissance (1626). The interior decoration of the church is dominated by the nine baroque side-altars, the work of Meinrad Guggenbichler (who also created the pulpit) and Franz Anton Koch. Worthy of particular attention is the elaborate doorway (1487) which leads to the sacristy on the north wall of the main choir. Above the sacristy lies the former library, in which the Austrian Museum of Pile Buildings and Folklore exhibits artefacts which bring to life the Mondsee culture and the history of the monastery (closed Monday). The wedding scene in *The Sound of Music* was filmed here, and not in Salzburg.

In the Mondsee Smoke House on an elevation behind the church, you can see the rural traditions of the area in an authentic setting. The **Church of Our Lady of Succour** (1455, converted to the baroque style in 1706) contains altars from the atelier of Meinrad Guggenbichler.

RECREATION AT MONDSEE

Mondsee, a holiday destination with a long tradition, offers a wide variety of sports and leisure activities. The lake, the warmest of all those in the Salzkammergut area, is 11 km (7 miles) long and some 2 km (1 mile) wide at its widest point; it is up to 70 m (230 ft) deep and is surrounded by the precipitous ramparts of the Drachenwand (1,000 m/3,280 ft) in the southwest and the Schafberg (1780 m/5,850 ft) in the south.

ATTERSEE

The best view of the Drachenwand and the Schlossberg is undoubtedly from the B151 along the northwest bank of the Mondsee. At **Unterach** (40 km/25 miles) you will reach the Attersee, the largest of the Salzkammergut lakes

Star Attraction
• Mondsee
  Monastery

Water Sports at Mondsee

If you enjoy water sports, then the closest lake offering a full range of activities is Mondsee. The possibilities are endless, from diving to surfing, yachting, fishing, water skiing and much more. On hot days the lakeside can become quite crowded, so make sure you get there early and book your activities. For more information contact the Mondsee Tourist Office on tel: (0043) 6232/2270 or visit www.mondsee.at

By the lake at Mondsee

Map on pages 46–47

The Salzkammergut

'Life is fun in the Salzkammergut' was the theme that echoed round Berlin in 1930 when Ralph Benatzky's operetta *The White Horse Inn* received its premiere. It helped to increase the international popularity of a region which in any case enjoyed an abundance of natural advantages. Some 40 lakes lie in a mountainous setting ranging from the gently rolling Alpine foothills via steep karst peaks to the glacial region of the Dachstein massif. This progression marks the north-south extension of the Salzkammergut, the borders of which are formed in the west by the peaks of the Osterhorn group and the Gosaukamm, and in the east by the Almtal, the Totes Gebirge and Grimming.

Wall mural at Unterach

(20 km/12 miles long, 3 km/2 miles wide and up to 171 m/561 ft deep). Sailing boats of all kinds scud across the surface, while in the water below you will find a great variety of fish, including trout which are served in local restaurants.

The lakeshore itself is ideal for holidays. There are long bathing beaches and, here and there, little villages which have lost none of their rural charm. In the south, the Attersee is framed by the Schafberg massif, the Leonsberg (1745 m/5,724 ft) and the steeply precipitous Höllen-Gebirge (1862 m/6,107ft); in the north, they fall away less steeply. Many pile dwellings and tools from the Stone Age have been found here. Signs of Roman occupation have also been discovered (for instance, the villas in Weyregg).

ATTERSEE VILLAGE

The hill on which the church stands forms the centre of the village of ★★ **Attersee** (pop. 1,500; 55 km/34 miles). It was formerly the site of an early medieval imperial palace, the *Atarnhova* (Attar's Court). When Henry II gave part of the Attergau to the archbishopric of Bamberg in 1007, it was converted into a fortified bishop's palace, which was subsequently sold in 1379 to the dukes of Austria. The latter then transferred their seat to the Koglberg near St Georgen *(see opposite page)* in the middle of the 15th century. The old castle, which since the 16th century had been in the possession of the counts of Khevenhüller, fell into disrepair. Between 1721–8 the count had the castle chapel rebuilt, transforming it into the baroque parish and pilgrimage church of Our Lady of the Assumption, also known as **Our Lady of Attersee**. It has been a prominent landmark, visible across the lake from afar ever since.

Below the church lie the beach and an adventure swimming pool, the lakeside promenade and an amusement park, all of which are popular with locals and visitors alike. *(For information about the town of Attersee and its surroundings contact the local tourist association, Nussdorferstrasse 15, A-4864 Attersee, tel: 07666-7719.)*

DETOURS AROUND ATTERSEE

An interesting detour to make from Attersee is to the parish church of **St Laurence** in the nearby village of **Abtsdorf**, which was under the jurisdiction of Mondsee Abbey until 1791, is a late-Gothic building with a baroque interior by Meinrad Guggenbichler (c1700).

Another stop-off could be made to the Buchberg. A nature trail has been laid out on the slopes of the Buchberg (810 m/2,860 ft). The footpath to **Berg** leads past the ruins of ancient and medieval defences built on the plateau of Castle Hill and on the top of the Buchberg.

St Georgen im Attergau (4 km/3 miles west of Attersee) has a village centre with stuccoed townhouses and a late-Gothic parish church (baroque high altar painting by Bartholomäus Altomonte, pulpit by Meinrad Guggenbichler). **Kogl Castle**, built in 1872, lies at the end of an avenue some 20 minutes from the centre of the village. Little remains of the former fortress on the Koglberg (670 m/2,190 ft, approximately one hour's walk).

WALCHEN CASTLE

An outing which will appeal to children in particular is the short trip on the narrow-gauge railway which runs from Attersee to **Walchen**

Star Attraction
•**Attersee**

Below: Attersee
Bottom: Unterach Lake

Map
on pages
46–47

Map
on pages
46–47

Tourism in Bad Ischl

At the beginning of the 19th century, a doctor in Ischl, Dr Josef Götz, first successfully employed brine in the treatment of miners suffering from gout and rheumatism. When, in 1822, the court physician Franz von Wirer learned of these techniques, he recommended to his noble patients that they should try it too and thus initiated the transformation of the little salt town into an aristocratic spa town. The best advertisement of all was Archduchess Sophie, who underwent treatment for infertility for the first time in Ischl in 1828, gave birth to the heir to the throne, Franz Joseph, in 1830, followed by his two brothers Maximilian and Ludwig – the 'Salt Princes', as they were popularly known.

Traditional hats

Castle (12 km/8 miles, before Vöcklamarkt). Here you will find a Children's World Museum which is designed to be as interactive as possible and encourages children to actually play with the exhibits.

KIENBACH VALLEY

A trip around the Attersee will permit you to make detours into a variety of valley landscapes. In Steinbach (23 km/14 miles from Attersee), a panoramic road leads off eastwards into the **Kienbach Valley**, continuing via Neukirchen (Hochkreuth Wildlife Park) to the Traunsee. From Weissenbach (27 km/17 miles from Attersee), the charming B153 road leads to **Bad Ischl** which is famed for the healing properties of the area's mineral salts. Over the years the town has grown wealthy and today it is one of the most well-known modern spa towns in Europe, with a range of luxury treatments and accommodation on offer.

Only the southern end of the Attersee and the village of Burgau (30 km/19 miles from Attersee) which actually belongs to Salzburg. The narrow climb up the Burggrabenklamm (entrance beside the Jägerwirt) ends in a rock cathedral with a waterfall which plunges downhill with particular force in spring when the snow has melted.

3: Opera and Emperors

Salzburg – St Gilgen – St Wolfgang – Bad Ischl – Bad Aussee (96 km/60 miles)

Map
on pages
46–47

This route leads into the heart of the Salzkammergut *(see page 51)*. You should leave Salzburg on the B158 *(see map, pages 46–47)*.

Apart from its popularity among visitors to Salzburg and the festival, **Hof** (pop. 2,800; 15 km/ 9 miles) is also a favourite starting-point for keen walkers. The village stretches out as far as Lake Fuschl (bathing beach). As you approach, but before the lake comes into view, on your left you will pass the **Jagdhof**, an old farmhouse which has been converted into a hotel; it also houses a hunting museum and pipe collection. From here you will have a view down to the lake and **Fuschl Castle**, which was once the hunting lodge and pleasure palace of the archbishops of Salzburg. At the eastern end of the 5 km (3 miles) lake, lies the attractive resort village of Fuschl (pop. 1,200), which has a bathing beach and a summer toboggan run.

Below: plaque outside Mozart's mother's house
Bottom: Wolfgangsee

WOLFGANGSEE

The most famous lake in the entire Salzkammergut, and a paradise for those who like watersports, is undoubtedly the **Wolfgangsee**. Eleven km (7 miles) long and 115 m (375 ft) deep, it is framed by mountains: the Schafberg (1,780 m/ 5,850 ft), the Zwölferhorn (1,520 m/4,990 ft) and the peaks of the Wieslerhorn (1,600 m/5,260 ft).

St Gilgen (pop. 3,000; 32 km/20 miles), the self-styled 'Mozart Village on the Wolfgangsee', lies on the northwest shore of the lake. The composer's mother was born here in the local courthouse, and his sister Nannerl also lived here for several years after her marriage. The village centre is a pedestrian zone, permitting a pleasant stroll past the pretty houses. The frescoes on the facade of the Hotel Post date from the 18th century. The little Folk Music Museum displays musical instruments from around the world. *(Information: Tourist Association, Mozartplatz 1, A-5340 St Gilgen, tel: 06227-2348.)*

Map
on pages
46–47

An attractive footpath leads from St Gilgen on the north shore of the lake, via Fürberg to the **Falkenstein**, a crag which falls precipitously down to the lake. If you continue along the same path through Ried, you will eventually come to St Wolfgang (the walk takes approximately three hours).

ABERSEE

Continuing by car along the B158, however, you will pass through **Abersee**. The lake itself once bore the same name which is now applied to the region on the southeast shore. There are a number of campsites on the spit of land jutting out into the lake and almost dividing it in two. It is not recommended that you make a day-trip to St Wolfgang by car, because it will probably be impossible to find a parking space when you get there. An alternative is to head for Abersee or Gschwendt, where you should leave the road and head for the lake. You can take the steamer across the lake to St Wolfgang from May to mid-October – an approach offering the added advantage of providing the best view of the village.

Michael Pacher

Michael Pacher is regarded as being one of the most important artists and wood carvers of the Late Gothic era. His main work is the altar in St Wolfgang's Church but he also carved a baroque high altar for the Fransiscan Church in Salzburg (where he died in 1489). Only the figure of the Virgin Mary with the Infant Christ remains as the centrepiece of Johann Bernhard Fischer von Erlach's altar in the Fransiscan Church.

ST WOLFGANG

St Wolfgang

★ **St Wolfgang** (pop. 2,800; 52 km/33 miles) achieved world fame through the operetta *The*

White Horse Inn (1930). As a result, the crowds of pilgrims of yore, who once came to pray at the Church of St Wolfgang, have nowadays been replaced by hordes of tourists. The saint was the archbishop of Regensburg, who, according to legend, withdrew to a cave on the Falkenstein, where he lived as a hermit to escape from Duke Henry the Quarrelsome of Bavaria. The village grew up around the church built here in his honour.

A fire destroyed the Romanesque church in 1429; the present building was constructed on the same site in three phases during the 15th/18th century. The interior houses one of the most famous masterpieces of late-Gothic art: the ★★★ **Pacher Altar** (1471–81). Michael Pacher, an artist and wood carver from South Tyrol, was responsible, together with artists from his atelier, for the carved shrine depicting the Coronation of the Virgin Mary, as well as for the pictures on the side-panels which, when open, depict the Nativity, the Circumcision of Christ and the Presentation of Jesus in the Temple, as well as the Death and Assumption of the Virgin Mary. The twin-altar produced by Thomas Schwanthaler (1676), an artist from the Innviertel, depicts the Holy Family on the left and St Wolfgang on the right; it is the church's most important baroque work of art. The pulpit and the three side-altars (1706) are the work of Meinrad Guggenbichler, the sculptor of Mondsee Monastery fame.

Other sites in St Wolfgang include a late-Gothic **pilgrim's fountain**, cast in 1515 and which stands on the terrace above the market square. The canopy is one of the earliest Renaissance monuments in Austria. The tall gabled houses (some of them several hundred years old) are crowded around the church and the market place.

The historic charm of the village is more in evidence on days when the streets are not full of tourists. Try to avoid visiting on Sundays, public holidays and during the holiday season. (*Information: Kurdirektion, Postfach 20, A-5360 St Wolfgang; tel: 06138-2239.*)

Star Attraction
• Pacher Altar

Below: Pilgrim's Fountain
Bottom: Pacher Altar

Map on pages 46–47

*Below: view from chairlift
Bottom: en route from
Bad Ischl to Bad Aussee*

THE SCHAFBERG

The ★ **Schafberg Railway** runs by rack and pinion and was built over 100 years ago. Some of the old steam engines still run from St Wolfgang between May and late October. On a clear day you can see the entire Salzkammergut from the Schafberg (1,780 m/5,850 ft). Beyond Strobl (pop. 3,200; gently sloping bathing beach), the road forks off to the Postalm (1,230 m/4,200 ft), the largest mountain plateau in Austria, with footpaths and good skiing amenities (downhill or cross-country).

★ **Bad Ischl** (pop. 13,000; 67 km/42 miles). The Old Town lies on a peninsula bordered by two rivers: the Ischl and the Traun. Bad Ischl was transformed from its hitherto Cinderella-like existence to the role of operetta princess during the first half of the 19th century, when the healing powers of the local mineral salts *(see page 54)* were made public. When the brine bathing institution opened in 1823, the number of guests totalled just 40. Only a few years later, the aristocracy from the court in Vienna came to take the waters at Bad Ischl, closely followed by everybody who was anybody.

IMPERIAL VILLA

The ★★ **former villa of Emperor Franz Joseph I** of Austria lies on the northern bank of the Ischl, and the villa once owned by Franz Lehár, the king

of operetta, on the south bank of the Traun. In 1853, Emperor Franz Joseph celebrated his betrothal to Princess Elizabeth of Bavaria ('Sissi') in Bad Ischl, in the former Hotel Austria.

Today the building houses the Municipal Museum, containing items relating to local folklore. Throughout his long life, the emperor spent virtually every summer in the imperial villa, a wedding present from his parents. It is an enlarged Biedermeier country mansion built in the shape of the letter 'E'. A tour of the living quarters, virtually unchanged since those days, provides an insight into the character of Franz Joseph. It was here, on 28 July 1914, that he reluctantly signed the ultimatum to Serbia – the prelude to World War I – one month after his nephew and heir, Franz Ferdinand, had been assassinated in Sarajevo. Thereafter, Franz Joseph never returned to Bad Ischl again. In the grounds of the imperial villa you will also see the Marble Palace of the Empress Elizabeth, which houses the Photographic Museum.

Star Attraction
• Imperial Villa

👁 **Habsburg Monarchy**
The Habsburg monarchy were the ruling house of Austria from 1282 to 1918. Through inter-marriage and wars, it encompassed land from Czechoslovakia, Poland and Hungary to Northern Italy, Spain to parts of France, the Netherlands and Germany. However, it did not incorporate the ecclesiastical principality of Salzburg until 1816. Luckily enough the Habsburg family did not spend much time in Salzburg city; they favoured the spas of Bad Ischl as a retreat instead. This lack of favour towards the city allowed the architecture to remain intact – otherwise Salzburg might have looked a little bit like Vienna or Budapest today.

ISCHL OPERETTAS

The Austro-Hungarian monarchy came to end in 1918, but the world of operetta lives on in Bad Ischl. It is maintained that the Hungarian composer Franz Lehár wrote 24 works for the stage here in the years between 1912–48. He bequeathed his villa to the town, keeping it in its original state, and opened it to the public as the Lehár Museum. In July and August each year, the Ischl Operettas recall the Golden Age of the little town.

You can enjoy a fine view from the summit of Siriuskogel (600 m/1,965 ft; chairlift), but even more magnificent is that from the Katrinalm (1,540 m/5,060 ft), from the top of which you can see further still. The Salzberg lies 3 km (2 miles) south of Bad Ischl. The mine, now no longer in operation, can be visited (slide, trip on pit railway, salt lake) and is good fun for children. *(Information: Bad Ischl Tourist Office, Bahnhofstrasse 6, A-4820, tel: 06132-27757–0.)*

Statue in garden of Franz Joseph's villa

Map on pages 46–47

Below: stag's head
Bottom: statue of Madonna

Traun Valley

Continuing along the B145 you will come to one of the most attractive sections of the Traun Valley, passing through Lauffen (70 km/44 miles; late-Gothic church of Our Lady of the Shadows) and Bad Goisern (pop. 7,000; 76 km/47 miles), with its iodine/sulphur spring. The Simonyaussicht beside the first major bend on the ascent to the Pötschen Pass (990 m/3,255 ft) provides a lovely view of the Hallstätter See.

Bad Aussee

★ **Bad Aussee** (pop. 5,100; 96 km/60 miles) is not only the centre of the Styrian Salzkammergut, but also of Austria itself. Fortunately it is only the geographical centre, otherwise it would not have remained a pretty little spa town. In the heart of Bad Aussee the building activities of the prosperous salt magnates and the Princely Salt Office are still in evidence. The foundations of the late Gothic Salt Office and Salt Chapel are said to date from the 14th century. Today they provide an attractive setting for the **Folklore Museum**.

In the parish church of **St Paul** (13th–15th-century, with two side-chapels dating from the 17th century), is a late-Gothic statue of the Virgin Mary of the 'Beautiful Madonna' type. Also of note is the **tabernacle**, which dates from 1523. The Chapel of the Holy Ghost adjoining the Market Hospital, built in 1395, contains two lovely Gothic winged altars. Opposite the church stands the birthplace of Anna Plochl (1804–85), daughter of the local postmaster and wife of Archduke John.

Spas and Cures

The market was founded by Duke Albert in 1290 when he had the princely salt works transferred here from Altaussee. Brine and saline mud have been used here for their curative properties for almost 150 years. More recent is the use of Glaubers salt for drinking cures. The spa centre has a covered swimming pool with brine mineral waters; the original spa house, built in 1870, has been allowed to fall into disrepair.

DETOURS

Apart from the road to **Altaussee** (pop. 1,900, 4 km/3 miles), there is also a footpath running beside the River Traun. The ★★ **Altausseer See** was once appropriately described as an inkwell in which numerous writers and composers dipped their quill pens. Johannes Brahms and Gustav Mahler, Hugo von Hofmannsthal, Arthur Schnitzler, Friedrich Torberg and many others found inspiration in the scenic beauty of the countryside. You will also find here a Via Artis circumventing the lake, providing information about the artists.

AUSSEER SEE

The salt storage complex at the Sandling (1,720 m/5,630 ft) is the largest in Austria. According to legend, the water sprite living in the lake pointed out the salt deposits to local inhabitants on their way to church. No wonder, then, that the deep green shimmering waters of the **Ausseer See** have inspired so many artists and has become the subject of many war-time myths. The beautiful lake is surrounded by the vertical rock face of the Trisselwand and the Loser (1,840 m/6,030 ft), along

Star Attraction
• **Altausseer See**

> **Walks**
> A walk along one of the sections of the Via Artis will provide a glimpse of the number of famous guests who visited Bad Aussee in the past, either to take the waters or to enjoy the refreshing climate in summer. Affixed to the historic buildings you will find plaques providing information about Hugo von Hofmannsthal, Nikolaus Lenau, Wilhelm Kienzl and others. A walk when the daffodils are out (mid-May until mid-June) leads across flower-bedecked meadows and slopes. The Daffodil Festival is held at the end of May/ beginning of June. *(Information: Oppauer Platz, A-8990 Bad Aussee, tel: 03622-52323.)*

Altaussee

Map
on pages
46–47

the rocky summit of which runs a panoramic road (toll; hang-gliding starting ramp; ski chairlift in winter (Sandling-Loser).

TOPLITZSEE

Footpaths lead from Altaussee (2 hours) and Bad Aussee (promenade, 1 hour) to the **Grundlsee** (6 km/4 miles long, 1 km/⅝ mile wide). The mountain walls enclosing the **Toplitzsee** on all sides are so steep that it is not possible to reach the lake by car. But a steamer trip on the lakes is in any case by far the best way to travel; you can embark in Gössl and sail on to the remote **Kammersee**, where one of the three sources of the Traun cascades downhill in a waterfall.

The Toplitzsee is so deep that it has attracted a number of stories around it that involve hidden treasure and adventure. It is said that at the end of World War II, a number of trunks containing the last of the Nazi gold reserves were thrown into the lake. The rumour that the famous 'amber room' was sunk here too gathered momentum when a submarine spotted cases with Russian lettering on them. It has not been possible to recover the trunks, so the secret remains locked inside them. One actual find though was a horde of forged pound notes that were supposed to be used to flood the English economy and to bring about the collapse of the country.

Below: parascending above the lake
Bottom: Altausseer See

4: Celts and Caves

Salzburg – Hallein – Golling – Lammertal – Abtenau – Hallstatt – Radstadt – Mauterndorf – Tamsweg – St Michael im Lungau (137 km/ 86 miles)

Map on pages 46–47

This winding route leads into the mountain (the salt mines at Hallein/Dürrnberg and Hallstatt), around the mountain (through the Lammertal and around the Tennengebirge), and beyond the mountain (across the Tauern Pass into the Lungau, whose inhabitants are locally known as 'the people from across the Tauern'). *(For more details, see maps on pages 46–47 and 64–65.)*

HALLEIN

Hallein (pop. 20,000; 15 km/9 miles) is the second-largest town in the province of Salzburg, the district capital of the Tennengau and an important industrial centre. It possesses an attractive town centre surrounded by the remains of the former fortifying walls. Hallein offers opportunities for a pleasant stroll, for the heart of the town is largely traffic-free. Some of the alleys date from the Middle Ages and are bordered by houses with baroque and rococo facades in a variety of colours. The parish church of **St Anthony the Hermit** has a Gothic choir and an early neoclassical nave (1769–75) designed by Wolfgang Hagenauer. The late-Romanesque tower burned down in 1943 and was rebuilt between 1965–6. Franz Xaver Gruber, the composer of *Silent Night, Holy Night (see page 48)*, was organist and choirmaster here. His grave is the only one to have remained when the adjoining cemetery was cleared away. To the north of the church you can also still see the house in which he lived.

Salt was once mined on the Dürrnberg (770 m/ 2,530 ft). Today, the excavations are aimed at the Celtic settlements which once stood here; successfully, too, as the Dürrnberg is the largest archaeological site for the investigation of Celtic culture. There is evidence that the Dürrnberg was settled as long ago as Neolithic times (*c*2000 BC).

Celtic Heritage
The Dürrnberg's most precious excavation today is not salt but artefacts from the Celtic settlements which once thrived there. Many valuable archeological finds can be found on display in the Hallein's open-air Celtic Museum along with a recreation of a farmstead complex.

Church of St Anthony the Hermit

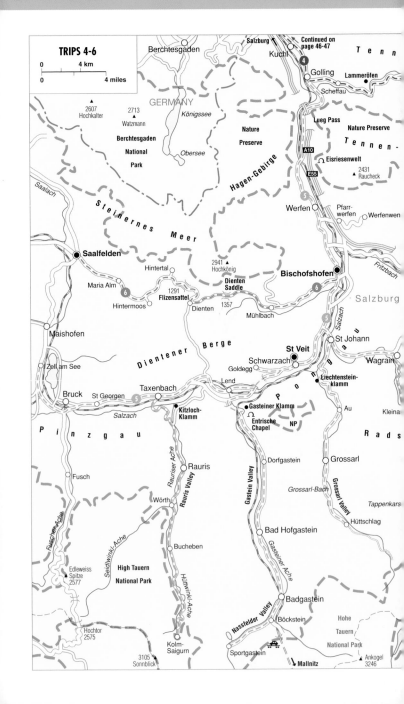

TRIPS 4-6

0   4 km

0   4 miles

Berchtesgaden

Salzburg

Kuchl

Continued on page 46-47

4

Golling

Lammeröfen

Scheffau

T e n n

GERMANY

▲ 2607 Hochkalter

▲ 2713 Watzmann

Königssee

Nature Preserve

Lueg Pass

Nature Preserve

Berchtesgaden National Park

Obersee

Hagen-Gebirge

T e n n e n -

A10

E55

Eisriesenwelt

▲ 2431 Raucheck

Saalach

S t e i n e r n e s   M e e r

Werfen

Pfarr-werfen

Werfenwen

Saalfelden

Hintertal

2941 ▲ Hochkönig

Dienten Saddle

Bischofshofen

Fritzbach

Maria Alm

6

1291 Flizensattel

Dienten

1357

Mühlbach

Salzburg

Hintermoos

D i e n t e n e r   B e r g e

6

Salzach

Maishofen

St Johann

St Veit

Schwarzach

Wagrain

Zell am See

Goldegg

Lend

Liechtenstein-klamm

P

Au

Kleina

Bruck

St Georgen

Taxenbach

5

o

n

g

Gasteiner Klamm

R a d s

P   i   n   z   g   a   u

Salzach

Kitzloch-Klamm

Entrische Chapel

NP

Fusch

Rauriser Ache

Rauris

Dorfgastein

Grossarl

Gastein Valley

Grossarl-Bach

Grossarl Valley

Tappenkars

Wörth

Hüttschlag

Seidlwinkl-Ache

Bucheben

Bad Hofgastein

Fuscher-Ache

High Tauern National Park

▲ Edelweiss Spitze 2577

Hüttwinkl-Ache

Gasteiner Ache

Badgastein

Nassfelder Valley

Böckstein

Hohe

Hochtor 2575

Tauern

National Park

3105 Sonnblick

Kolm-Saigurn

Sportgastein

Mallnitz

Ankogel 3246

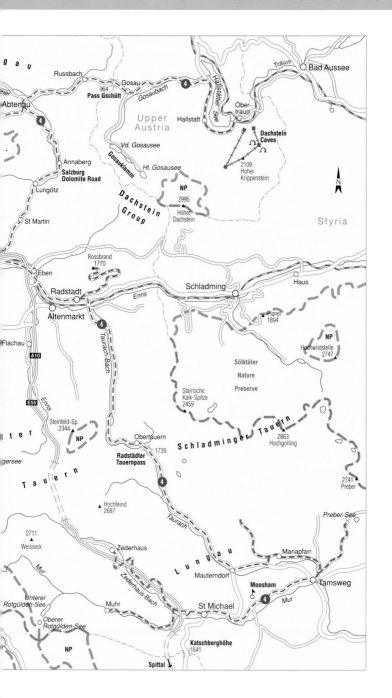

Map on pages 46–47

Red Marble

Near the quiet holiday resort of Adnet, which lies about 2 km (1 mile) from Hallein, is the place where red Adnet marble is quarried before being used for a large number of works of art. There is also an educational trail and a small museum here.

Relic at the Celtic Museum

Settlements grew up here during the late Hallstatt era and the La Tène era (600 BC until the birth of Christ). Some 200 years before Christ, the mining stopped and the inhabitants moved away. At the end of the 12th century, salt production started up again and became one of the important sources of income of the prince-bishops of Salzburg. It was only a few years ago that the last miner descended the mine shaft; in 1989 the mine (which had produced 40,000 tonnes of salt annually) closed because it was no longer economically viable.

Hallein's Celtic Museum

Hallein's ★★ **Celtic Museum** exhibits the valuable archaeological finds, including tools and equipment used by the early miners, as well as priceless burial gifts. The museum is housed in the former administrative building (1654) of the mining and salt works commission of the prince-bishops; other sections are devoted to the history of the town and local customs and guilds.

There is a road leading up the Dürrnberg, but you can also ascend the mountain by cable car; the valley station is on the southern edge of town. The open-air Celtic Museum includes a reconstruction of a farmstead complex and a grave. A Celtic information trail completes the exhibition. The disused ★ **salt mine** offers a ride in the pit train, **slides**, a 90-m (295-ft) illuminated salt lake and underground display rooms showing evidence of mining activities in early historic times. The last remaining brine cavern (1704) contains a mining museum.

Bad Dürrnberg

Local salt is used for its curative properties in Bad Dürrnberg, which since 1938 has formed part of the town of Hallein. The parish church of the **Assumption of the Virgin Mary** is also a pilgrimage church; it was built in 1594–1612 of locally quarried, distinctive reddish-coloured marble. (*Information: Hallein Tourist Office, Mauttorpromernade; tel: 06245-85394.*)

GOLLING

Golling (pop. 3,800, 28 km/18 miles), underwent a major restoration programme in honour of its 750-year anniversary in 1991. The pretty village centre attracts many visitors, and has a number of little gardens on the pavement, locally known as *Schanigärten*.

Food for thought is provided in the interesting Folklore Museum in the castle, which is really a fortress (the oldest sections date from the 13th century). In an oasis of green to the southwest, in the district known as Torren, stands the former pilgrimage church of St Nicholas on a rocky eminence. Here, too, you will find the entrance to the valley, where the **Golling waterfall** cascades over a 76-m (250-ft) precipice.

The B162 forks off eastwards into the ★★**Lammertal**, the most spectacular section of which begins past Oberscheffau. Here is the entrance to the Lammeröfen, a remarkable natural phenomenon consisting of a gorge 2 km (1 mile) long and 60 m (200 ft) wide. A well-constructed footpath leads along the overhanging rock walls, in some places very close to the water. If you want to experience the spray from even closer quarters, you will find the Lammertal is a great challenge for all canoeing and rafting enthusiasts.

Star Attractions
• **Celtic Museum**
• **The Lammertal**

Below: Golling waterfall
Bottom: Castle at Golling

Map on pages 46–47

ABTENAU

Abtenau (pop. 5,300; 39 km/24 miles), has specialised in a variety of sports. Two clubs offer canoeing, rafting, paragliding and hang gliding, wild-water swimming, mountain biking, etc. Some 100 km (63 miles) of marked footpaths will appeal to the rucksack brigade. In winter, the most popular winter sports centre in the Tennengau forms a cornerstone of the West Dachstein ski region (195 km/122 miles of pistes). The Postalm *(see page 118)* is also nearby. *(Information: Tourist Office, Markt 165, A-5441 Abtenau, tel: 06243-22140.)*

The man in the salt

Found in 1734, this well-preserved body was thought to be around 100 years old and was duly buried in the graveyard in Hallstatt. It was only much later, during other excavation work, that it became apparent that the 'salted devil' was probably far older than originally estimated.

A DETOUR TO HALLSTATT

If you carry on through the Russbach Valley and across the Gschütt Pass (964 m/3,162 ft), you will arrive in **Gosau** (pop. 1,900). Here you must decide whether to continue in a southerly or an easterly direction. If you go south, following the Gosau Brook upstream towards its source, you will first reach the Lower Gosausee (20 km/13 miles). The Dachstein glaciers reflect in the water here, a theme which is featured in every photo album of the region. The Gosauklamm cable car leads up to the Gablonzer Hütte on the Zwieselalm, 1,520 m (4,990 ft); refreshments are available in summer. The path to the

Hallstatt

Upper Gosausee (accessible only on foot) takes just under 2 hours.

If, however, you continue eastwards along the B166, you will eventually reach Lake Hallstatt.

HALLSTATT

★★ **Hallstatt** (pop. 1,200), lies 27 km (17 miles) from the junction. 'I have never in my life seen a village with as unusual a setting as Hallstatt. The houses appear to cling to the steep, narrow lake shore, and it seems as if a minor earthquake is all that would be necessary to tip the entire market place into the waters of the lake,' was the apprehensive comment by the travel writer Franz Sartori in 1813. Until 1890, Hallstatt could be reached only by boat or along mule tracks, and on the market place often the only way of getting from one house to the next was via the upper storeys or the roof trusses.

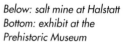

Below: salt mine at Halstatt
Bottom: exhibit at the Prehistoric Museum

Nowadays there are streets, but it is still advisable to leave your car in the first parking space you can find, as cars are not allowed in the town proper.

Hallstatt has every right to consider itself the true heart of the Salzkammergut. In prehistoric times, the vital mineral, salt, was mined in the Salzberg. The discovery of the Celtic burial ground in the mid-19th century led to the Early Iron Age (c800–400 BC) being christened the Hallstatt era. The finds can be viewed in the ★★★ **Prehistoric Museum**. It is possible that salt mining came to a halt during Roman times, but by the Middle Ages it had been revived. In 1284 Duke Albert had Rudolf's Tower built at an altitude of 855 m (2,800 ft) to protect the mines, naming it after his father. In 1311 his consort Elisabeth gave the little community market rights.

The ★ **salt mines** are still in operation. You can easily make the ascent to the Upper Salzberg Valley (840 m/2,750 ft) by cable car. This is the site of the burial ground (approximately 2,000 graves) and the entrance to the mine itself. The conducted tour includes an

Map
on pages
46–47

explanation of the various methods of salt extraction: the salt lake is reached by means of long slides; the return trip back to the daylight is by mining truck.

OUR LADY OF ASSUMPTION

Hallstatt's Gothic parish church of **Our Lady of the Assumption** has an unusual floor plan. The winged altar, thought to be by Lienhart Astl (1515), is on a par with the Pacher Altar in St Wolfgang *(see page 56)*. The charnel house behind the church provides visual proof that, until a few years ago, the village did not even have sufficient room for its dead: after 10 years the graves were cleared and the bones – often artistically painted – were stacked in the charnel house. The **Local History Museum** is housed in the oldest secular building in Hallstatt (14th-century). Each year, the Corpus Christi procession is held in boats on the lake. *(Information: Tourist Association, Seestrasse 169, A-4830 Hallstatt, tel: 06134-8208.)*

Above Obertraun (4 km/3 miles from Hallstatt) lies the valley station of the Dachstein cable car to the Hoher Krippenstein (2,110 m/6,920 ft; karst nature trail, 2 hours). Above the middle station (1,350 m/4,430 ft) lie the entrances to the ★★ **Dachstein Caves**. The Mammoth's Cave (37 km/23 miles long, 1,180 m/3,870 ft deep) leads into the bizarre forked 'cathedrals' with eerily beautiful names like 'The Kingdom of Shadows' or 'The Hall of Forgetfulness'. The vast Ice Cave (a conducted tour takes 1 hour) is one of Austria's great natural wonders, like the Eisriesenwelt Caves near Werfen *(see page 77)* There are bizarre towers and ice waterfalls in the rocky grottoes.

GOSAU GORGE

East of Abtenau, the B166 turns southwards. This section through the Lammertal is known as Salzburg's Dolomite Road; the massive Gosau Gorge in the east with its sea of craggy, whiteish

Dachstein Giant Ice Caves
These caves are millions of years old; however, the ice has only been forming here for about 500 years. The ice freezes in the winter and then melts in the summer. At some points, the ice is over 25 m (80 ft) thick. There are some unusual and beautiful formations such as the 'Ice Chapel', King Arthur's, Parisifal's and Tristan's Domes. The caves are open to visitors from May to October.

Local History Museum

jagged peaks certainly supports the comparison. The little villages (Annaberg, Lungötz, St Martin) have never attracted large numbers of visitors. In summer they are ideal starting-points for walkers, and in winter for cross-country and downhill skiers (Dachstein West Ski Region).

RADSTADT

Radstadt (pop. 4,000; 70 km/43 miles) grew up in the late 13th century as a little town on a rocky terrace on the banks of the River Enns; its purpose was to defend the boundary to Styria and the trade route through the Taurach Valley. The circular town wall with its three watch-towers (16th century) is still virtually intact, as is the original street layout. The medieval buildings were destroyed in a number of fires; only one house (Hoheneckgasse 6) and the parish church of **Our Lady of the Assumption**, dating from Romanesque and Gothic times, are still in existence. A late-Gothic light column (1513), known as the Cobbler's Column, stands in the graveyard.

The name Radstadt is known to ski enthusiasts all around the world. The Radstadt-Altenmarkt ski complex is part of the Amadé Sports World *(see page 119)*. *(Information: Tourist Association, Stadtplatz 17, A-5550 Radstadt, tel: 06452-7472.)*

(see page 119)

Star Attraction
• **Dachstein Caves**

Below: road to the Tauern Pass
Bottom: Church of Our Lady of the Assumption

Map
on pages
64–65

Below: the Tauern Pass
Bottom: Mauterndorf Castle

OBERTAUERN

The B99 follows the route of the former Roman road along the Taurach Valley before climbing up to the Tauern Pass (1,740 m/5,700 ft; 91 km/ 57 miles). Shortly before you reach the top you will come to **Obertauern** (pop. 700). This hamlet was also more or less planned, albeit not until the 20th century. The lack of buildings of architectural merit is of little concern to the countless holidaymakers who come for the skiing; their one interest is the varied terrain with an absolute guarantee of snow from November until May, 150 km (95 miles) of prepared pistes and 26 ski-lifts.

The border of the Lungau runs through Obertauern. This district seems to have little in common with the rest of the Salzburger Land. The high-altitude basin is surrounded by mountain peaks and is accessible only via Styria and the Mur Valley.

This isolation has helped to preserve much of the original character and customs of the district and its people. The villages have been spared defacement by the over-precipitous construction of hotels and holiday homes. A rich cultural tradition has been preserved, including the Corpus Christi procession in Zederhaus and Muhr, not far from St Michael, and the Samson Procession *(see pages 13–14)*.

MAUTERNDORF

Mauterndorf (pop. 1,600; 110 km/70 miles) is dominated by its ★★ **castle**. Looking at first glance like a giant toy, it was built by the Cathedral Chapter of Salzburg in 1253 to protect the valley and the village. Today the castle is a cultural centre and houses the **Lungau Regional Museum**, which has an interesting array of exhibits. The castle chapel dates from 1339 and boasts the oldest Gothic frescoes in the Salzburg region (1350), as well as a winged altar dating from 1452. The name of the village, Mauterndorf, reveals the fact that the settlement had the right to levy tolls (from 1143), thus making it the oldest customs post in the eastern Alpine region. It lies on what since Roman times had been one of the important trade routes to Italy. In 1217 the village also acquired market rights. The townhouses with their stepped gables (16th–17th century) surrounding the market place (a rarity in the Alpine regions) bear witness to the steadily increasing prosperity of this attractive town.

To the west of the village is a cable car leading to the Speiereckhütte, the starting-point for mountain walks and the ski arena Speiereck-Grosseck. (*Information: Tourist Association, A-5570 Mauterndorf, tel: 06472-7949.*)

MARIAPFARR

Mariapfarr (pop. 2,300; 114 km/70 miles) is blessed with regards to its location. A holiday resort can wish for nothing better than to be situated in the sunniest corner of the entire country, in a lovely geographical setting. Not content with that, Mariapfarr can also lay claim to the **oldest church** in the Lungau to be listed in historical records (923). There is some doubt as to whether the church in question really is the parish church of Our Lady of the Assumption, but there is nonetheless no question of its great age and artistic merit. The original choir – later rebuilt as the bay of the present choir – has a tower (1220) and a cycle of frescoes portraying the Life of Christ. The present altar area was added towards

Star Attraction
• Mauterndorf Castle

Walking Guide Books
Hiking and walking publications to Salzburg include the *Arno Trail Guidebook*, which covers the 1,200 km (746 miles) of Salzburg's borders and the *Salzburg Hiking Atlas* featuring 10 trekking tours. Both publications are available from the regional tourist board.

Speiereckhütte

Map
on pages
64–65

Lake Preber

Lake Preber, 8 km/5 miles north of Tamsweg, is surrounded by meadows and woods. Here, on the last weekend in August, a remarkable shooting contest takes place in which experts face an unusual challenge. They must aim not directly at the targets, but at the targets' reflections in the water of the lake.

the end of the 14th century; St George's Chapel dates from about 1430. Both still display their original frescoes.

Tamsweg

Tamsweg (pop. 5,000; 125 km/80 miles), is the regional capital of the Lungau. Thanks to its corner towers, the town hall (1570) on the market place may look like a miniature castle, but was in fact previously a townhouse. The former palace of the Kuenberg family (1742–9) lies in the Kirchengasse, as does St Barbara's Hospital. Originally built as a home for elderly and sick miners, today it houses the Lungau Regional Museum.

The Church of St Leonard

It seems unlikely that the statue of St Leonard would have absconded from its setting, as it reputedly did in 1421. The saint mysteriously disappeared three times from the earlier church building, and was found on each occasion under a juniper bush on an eminence on the outskirts of the village. This was interpreted as a sign that St Leonard wished the villagers to build a new church there; between 1424–33, construction went ahead on a late-Gothic masterpiece which was surrounded by a fortifying wall in 1480. The site of ★ **St Leonard's** is, indeed, superb: visible from afar, the little church soars above the treetops of the surrounding woodland. It became one of the most important pilgrimage churches in Austria and is famous for its valuable interior, especially the stained-glass windows, the colours of which are particularly vivid. (*Information: Tourist Association, 107 Church Lane, A-5580 Tamsweg, tel: 06477-2145.*)

Church of St Leonard

★★ **Moosham Castle**, on the B96, was first mentioned in records in 1256. Originally a courthouse, its main business was concerned with the prosecution of men and women suspected of being witches and wizards; it possesses a torture chamber as well as rooms with period furnishings. Today there is also a castle tavern where visitors can find refreshment during their visit.

ST MICHAEL IM LUNGAU

St Michael im Lungau (pop. 3,400; 137 km/86 miles) has a remarkable concentration of churches with interesting wall paintings: the parish church of **St Michael** possesses remains of frescoes dating from the first half of the 13th–17th century; there is also a Roman gravestone in the North Porch. The neighbouring **Chapel of St Wolfgang** in the former charnel house has Gothic frescoes. The sister church of **St Martin** in the suburb of the same name boasts a cycle of frescoes on the north outside wall dating from the first half of the 15th century; **St Anne's Chapel**, in the former charnel house, is adorned with late-Gothic wall paintings. The Gothic church of **St Giles** has a portrait of St Christopher dating from about 1400. In winter, the village's sporting amenities include well-prepared ski pistes and a 50-km (30-mile) cross-country ski trail through the Mur Valley. In summer you will find 150 km (94 miles) of marked footpaths. *(Information: Tourist Association, Raikaplatz, A-5582 St Michael im Lungau, tel: 06477-8913.)*

Star Attraction
• Moosham Castle

Below: detail of frescoes in St Martin's Church
Bottom: Moosham Castle

Map
on pages
64–65

Hohenwerfen

Located in Werfen, south of Salzburg Hohenwerfen castle was originally built in 1077 for the archbishop of Salzburg. Local folklore states that it took over 400 years to finish and this becomes clear on inspection. It is truly impregnable. An exceptionally impressive castle, it sits on the top of a cliff surrounded by rugged mountain ranges. A steep path leads to the castle. The dungeons, archer emplacements and the infallible network of walls can still be visited.

According to folklore the dungeons in these castles were used and filled to capacity with the "unwanted sorts" according to the Archbishops of Salzburg, such as missionaries who were spreading news about Protestantism – it is thought that these men were locked up in the darkness in solitary confinement for years and only set free when they had gone mad. The castle might seem familiar, as it was used in the film *Where Eagles Dare*.

5: Into the Valleys

Werfen – St Johann im Pongau – Kleinarl and Grossarl Valleys – Lend – Gastein Valley – Taxenbach – Rauris Valley – Zell am See (104 km/ 65 miles)

Trip 5 follows the Salzach Valley, which runs in an east-west direction beyond St Johann , collecting four of the most attractive valleys of the High Tauern on its way: the valleys of the Kleinarl and the Grossarl, the Gastein Valley and the Rauris Valley (*see map, pages 64–65*).

WERFEN

South of Golling (28 km/18 miles; for a description of the route between Salzburg and Golling see Trip 4, *page 65*), the Salzach Valley suddenly becomes much narrower. The B159 follows the old Roman Road over the Lueg Pass (550 m/1,810 ft). Here the river has buried itself deeply between the Hagen Mountains and the Tennengebirge, forming the Salzachöfen, a gorge some 1½ km (1 mile) long, accessible via a footpath leading down from the Lueg Pass. **Werfen** (pop. 3,500, 44 km/28 miles). When, in 1077, Archbishop Gebhard took sides with the Pope against the emperor in the Investiture Dispute, he also undertook comprehensive measures to protect his capital city. In the same year he began building fortresses in Salzburg, Werfen and Friesach (Carinthia).

Hohenwerfen:
where eagles still dare

HOHENWERFEN

The steep rocky outcrop (680 m/2,230 ft) in the Salzach Valley was a perfect site for a castle to protect the Lueg Pass, which was crossed by the road from the south, from attack by the imperial armies. Extensions during the 12th–16th century transformed **Hohenwerfen** into the fairy tale fortress it still resembles today. Major renovation was necessary following a fire in 1931. Today the castle is the setting for cultural events and conferences (conducted tours; bird station with birds of prey and demonstrations with eagles, vultures

and falcons once or twice a day). *(Information: Tourist Association, Markt 35, A-5450 Werfen, tel: 06468-5388.)*

Star Attraction
•Eisriesenwelt Caves

EISRIESENWELT

The ★★ **Eisriesenwelt Caves**, the 'World of the Ice Giants', is thought to be the world's largest ice cave: a network of caves extending over more than 47 km (29 miles). It is a fairy-tale world in which figures from Nordic mythology provide the names for the ice formations created when the melting snow froze: the Hymir Hall, Frigga's Veil and Odin's Room. There is a vast ice cathedral named after the explorer of the caves, Alexander von Mork (1887–1914), who was also buried here.

Below: Bischofshofen
Bottom: fortress at Werfen

The cave was explored for the first time in 1879. Only a small section (under a km) of the entire system is open to the public. You should wear warm clothing and stout shoes. The caves are a 15-minute walk from the carpark (6 km/4 miles north of Werfen). Conducted tours, which take place from May to early October, take about 1½ hours; June and September 9am–3.30pm, July to August 9am–4.30pm.

Bischofshofen (pop. 10,000, 53 km/33 miles) lies straddled across the hollow in the Salzach Valley between the mouth of the Fritzbach and the Mühlbach. The home of the Epiphany ski-jump-

Map on pages 64–65

Below: ornate Bischofshofen doorway
Bottom: road to the Grossarl Valley

ing contest, held within the framework of the Vier-Schanzen Tournament in early January, has spread itself out across a setting rich in history. The region has been settled since Neolithic times. In 700, St Rupert founded a monk's cell dedicated to St Maximilian. The Gothic parish church of **St Maximilian** was built around a Romanesque core; the marble tomb of Bishop Sylvester of Chiemsee is ascribed to Hans Baldauf (1453), and is the only extant Gothic raised tomb in the Salzburg region. The famous Cross of St Rupert (the original of which is preserved in the priest house) was made in Ireland in about 700 and was probably brought to Salzburg under St Virgil.

OTHER SIGHTS

Also of interest in Bischofshofen are the **Kastenhof**, a Romanesque residential tower standing beside the parish church, and the Gothic church of the **Virgin Mary**, also built round an originally Romanesque structure. *(Information: Tourist Association, Salzburger Strasse 1, A-5500 Bischofshofen, tel: 06462-2471.)*

St Johann im Pongau (pop. 8,900; 63 km/39 miles) was destroyed by a fire in 1855, but no expense was spared with the reconstruction. The heart of the new settlement is a massive neo-Gothic Church. Constructed in the historic style,

it was nicknamed the **Pongau Cathedral**. The town forms the core of the extensive Amadé Sports World (120 lifts, 320 km/200 miles of pistes). Every year at the Feast of the Epiphany (6 January), the ancient tradition known as the *Pongauer Pertchenlauf* is held in St Johann *(see page 78). (Information: Tourist Association, Engineer Ludwigpitchstrasse 1, A-5600 St Johann im Pongau, tel: 06412-60360.)*

KLEINARL VALLEY

The holiday and winter sports resort of Wagrain (pop. 3,000) lies 8 km (5 miles) east of St Johann. It marks the beginning of the **Kleinarl Valley**. From the Jägersee (1,100 m/3,600 ft) a gravel road leads for 4 km (3 miles) to the Schwabalm, where you will have to park your car. If you continue into the valley on foot, however, you will be rewarded with a view of the picturesque Tappenkarsee (1,760m/5,780ft); refreshments are available during the summer months (mid-June until September) in the Tappenkarseehütte restaurant. You should not go swimming or diving in this lake, as it is said to be bottomless. The round-trip from the Jägersee takes approximately 6 hours.

GROSSARL VALLEY

The **Grossarl Valley** lies 5 km (3 miles) due south of St Johann. Its entrance is guarded by the mighty ramparts of the Liechtensteinklamm, one of the most impressive gorges in the entire eastern Alps. The path through the gorge, which in some places is only 2 m (7 ft) wide, ends after about 30 minutes' walk beside a 50-m (160-ft) high waterfall. **Grossarl** (pop. 3,400; 15 km/9 miles from St Johann) is a popular destination for mountain walkers in summer and for skiers in winter (Dorfgastein-Grossarl: 80 km/50 miles of pistes, 40 km/25 miles of cross-country tracks). At the end of the valley lies the village of Hüttschlag (pop. 900), whose name recalls the region's mining past. A selection of imposing farmhouses and the beautiful parish church (1679) cluster together to form a rural idyll.

Flachau
Flachau is the World Cup Ski Resort and home to World Champion skier, Hermann Maier. Here you will find the Hermann Maier Ski School where you can learn to ski in his style.

Grossarl

Map on pages 64–65

Gastein Mineral Water

The water that gushes from the springs in Bad Gastein, has a high radium and radon content, which makes it particularly effective in curing rheumatic diseases and inflammations. People have known about its powers for around 5,000 years. In the Middle Ages, public baths were built. In 1621, Paris Lodron forbade mixed bathing in the baths, as it was thought to be 'lewd'. Paracelsus, the great Salzburg physician was well aware of the water's properties, but even he was unable to ascribe their origin. It was only in the 20th century, when Marie Curie discovered radium, that the puzzle was solved.

GOLDEGG

A few kilometres south of St Johann, the Salzach Valley bends to follow an east-west direction, which means that the villages on the southern edge of the Dienten Mountains bask in sunshine from morning till evening. Accordingly, this medium-altitude region has been christened 'the sun terraces of the Pongau'; the principal villages are Schwarzach (pop. 3,500) and St Veit (pop. 3,000; 70 km/44 miles), the first place in the Salzburg region to be classified as a health resort (1989) by virtue of its climate. Goldegg, in particular, has a pretty location on this mountain terrace, lying on the shores of a moorland lake (therapeutic baths). **Goldegg Castle** can trace its origins back to a building dating from 1323; over the years it underwent reconstruction on a number of occasions and has recently been meticulously restored. The Knights' Hall has wood panelling dating from about 1500 and frescoes from 1536, which make it the most important example of interior decoration dating purely from this era in the Salzburg region. Today, the castle houses the Pongau Museum of Local History.

DETOUR TO THE GASTEIN VALLEY

Near Lend (80 km/50 miles), the B167 forks off into the **Gastein Valley**, which has enjoyed a certain degree of celebrity since the Middle Ages. The gold mines have long since closed down, but the healing powers of the bubbling mineral springs continue uninterrupted, increasing not only the wellbeing of the visitors, but also the prosperity of the local residents. The Gasteiner Ache completes its course towards the Salzach with a great deal of turbulence as it rushes through the Gastein Gorge. Perched up above the medieval **Klammstein Castle** (conducted tours) not far to the south stands the **Entrische Kirche**, one of the largest stalagmite caves in the Central Alps; during the Counter-Reformation it was used by Protestants as a secret place of worship. From Klammstein carpark on the B167 a footpath with a nature trail leads to the cave entrance (40-minute walk; conducted tours mid-March to mid-October).

Goldegg Castle

GASTEIN VALLEY

The first village in the valley is **Dorfgastein** (pop. 1,500), 9 km (6 miles) from Lend. There are plenty of opportunities to satisfy sporting enthusiasts in summertime: riding, hang gliding, parasailing, rafting and sunbathing and even more in winter, with the skiing at Grossarl-Dorfgastein.

Bad Hofgastein (pop. 6,000), 17 km (11 miles) from Lend, offers the infrastructure of a large resort town with an Alpine Spa Gardens, at the centre of which stands the modern spa and leisure complex. There is an indoor pool (mineral water) and a wide variety of treatments to regenerate the body, spirit and soul. The Alpen Therme Gastein in Bad Hofgastein offers the best in health and leisure as well as a panoramic view of the glacier world of the Hohe Tauern National Park. Some of the highlights include the Relax World, the Family World with adventure slides and the Gusto World where you can enjoy healthy eating with a panoramic view.

★★**Bad Gastein** (pop. 5,600), 25 km (16 miles) from Lend, is the most famous town in the valley. As long ago as the Middle Ages it was popular as a health resort. Gastein became a spa town during the second half of the 19th century, when members of the Habsburg and Hohenzollern dynasties and the crowned heads of distant

Star Attraction
• **Bad Gastein**

Below: spa sign
Bottom: indoor pool at Bad Hofgastein

Map on pages 64–65

countries came in hordes, staying until the 1960s, when international celebrities began to seek amusement elsewhere. There is also a casino, and for winter sports fans the **Schlossalm-Stubnerkogel ski area**. The town itself is also an attraction, having grown up around the mighty waterfall of the Gasteiner Ache. *(Information: Spa and Tourist Association, Kaiser-Franz-Josef-Strasse 27, A-5640 Bad Gastein, tel: 06434-25310.)*

Below: Böckstein
Bottom: Bucheben

BÖCKSTEIN

Böckstein lies in the upper reaches of the Gastein Valley. Here, the region's past importance as a major mining centre can be observed cheek by jowl with the present reality of a modern resort. The ancient residential and industrial complex dating from the 18th century has been preserved in its entirety. The pilgrimage church of **Our Lady of Good Counsel** was built between 1764–1767.

It was only in 1940 that the therapeutic value of the radon-rich air in the former mining galleries (38–41°C/100–106°F; humidity 75–95 percent) was discovered during attempts to revive the gold-mining industry. The toll road continues to the Nassfeld, where you will find the Sportgastein ski-lift complex. The Tauern tunnel (9 km/5 miles) begins here. Only 8km (5 miles) west

of Lend, near Taxenbach (pop. 3,000), lies the entrance to the next main valley, through which the River Salzach flows.

Star Attraction
• Rauris Valley

DETOUR TO THE RAURIS VALLEY

On the last stage of its journey towards the Salzach, the Rauriser Ache (like the Gastein) has to squeeze its way between high rock faces, passing the Kitzloch Gorge, which has a waterfall and stalagmite cave.

Gold mining was once an important economic force in the ★★ **Rauris Valley**, a fact to which the 15th/16th century workers' cottages in **Rauris** (pop. 3,000, 10 km/6 miles from Taxenbach) testify. The **Museum of Local History** in the former schoolhouse (1563) provides an insight into the valley, its plant and animal life and its history. The **parish church** has a tower and choir dating from late Gothic times (1510–16), while the nave was built between 1774–1780. **St Michael's Chapel** was built in 1497. In contrast to the Gastein Valley, both the village of Rauris and its surrounding valley have largely retained their rural tranquillity. Even in winter the bustle around the nine ski-lifts (30 km/19 miles) is still comparatively gentle. In summer, Rauris is the gateway to a veritable paradise for mountain walks. *(Information: Tourist Association, Marktplatz 30, A-5661 Rauris, tel: 06544-6237.)*

The pretty village of Rauris

BUCHEBEN

In **Wörth** (14 km/9 miles from Taxenbach), the valley forks into two. A mule path which was of great importance during the Middle Ages leads along the Seidlwinkl Ache to the Hochtor (2,575 m/8,446 ft; 6 hours). In the Hüttwinkl Valley, on the other hand, you can reach **Bucheben** only 5 km (3 miles) later. Its **parish church** and neighbouring **priest house** (both built in 1785), the tavern building and the Kirchenwirt form a picturesque ensemble, the setting for the **Rauris Festival of Literature** each spring. In **Kalm-Saigurn** at the far end of the valley (16 km/

Map
on pages
64–65

Europa Sport Region
This varied and scenically impressive skiing region encompasses the resorts of Zell am See and Kaprun. There are over 350 km (217 miles) of pistes, 100 lifts and four mountains to explore. Because of the glacier on the Kitzsteinhorn, you can enjoy all-year-round skiing here.

10 miles from Wörth) you can explore the ruins of the mining installations and the miners' cottages along the Tauerngold Circular Footpath (it takes three hours to walk the entire length, including the Sonnblick glacier nature trail).

ZELL AM SEE

The final destination along this route is **Zell am See** (pop. 9,700, 100km/60 miles). It became a popular summer resort after the construction of the railway line at the end of the 19th century. The town's charming location on the alluvial headland jutting out into the lake and the attractive walking country were the main attractions. Even Emperor Francis Joseph climbed to the top of the Schmittenhöhe (1,965 m/6,445 ft), the famous lookout mountain. Today a cable car provides a much easier approach. In addition to the natural attractions, there are also a comprehensive range of sporting and leisure facilities, including a 27-hole golf course and a gliding school. In winter, the town forms the centre of the European Sport Region Kaprun-Zell am See, including the local mountains, the Schmittenhöhe and the Kitzsteinhorn (3,203 m/10,506 ft; 130 km/80 miles of pistes; 300 km/188 miles of cross-country tracks).

OTHER SIGHTS

Zell am See, today the district capital of the Pinzgau, was built during the 8th century as a monk's cell, as its name indicates. Three buildings represent what is left of the old heart of the town. **Rosenberg Castle** (1583) is the town hall today, whilst the **Bailiff's Tower** – an old defensive tower thought to date from the 13th century – houses the Museum of Local History. The Parish Church of **St Hippolytus** was originally a Romanesque-Gothic basilica which was later rebuilt; of particular charm is the organ loft (1514–5), with elegant net vaulting and fine tracery; it is supported by pillars of Adnet marble. (*Information: Spa Administrative Offices, Brucker Bundesstrasse 1, A-5700 Zell am See, tel: 06542-7700.*)

Bailiff's Tower

6: Peaks and Slopes

Bischofshofen – Dienten – Saalfelden (45 km/ 30 miles)

Map on pages 64–65

The panorama of the Dienten Mountains and the Steinernes Meer forms the central attraction of the picturesque route described below. It is advisable to choose a fine day for this trip so that you can enjoy the views and make good use of your camera *(see map, pages 64–65)*.

Close to Bischofshofen *(see page 77)*, the **Mühlbach Valley** opens up. Copper was mined in Mühlbach itself (pop. 1,600; 9 km/6 miles) until 1977. The Mining Museum and Demonstration Copper Mine provide an insight into this former industry (opening times vary; for information, tel: 06467-7235).

Below: boarding on the slopes
Bottom: picture postcard views on road to Arthurhaus

THE HOCHKÖNIG

The imposing limestone massif of the ★ **Hochkönig** (2,940 m/9,650 ft) includes a glacial plateau. A legend relates the origins of its name, the Flooded Meadow. In order to punish the wanton inhabitants of these rich pastures, who lived in luxury but refused a beggar a piece of bread, a thunderbolt struck the fertile meadowland and covered it with ice. You will have no problems viewing the steep slopes of the

Map
on pages
64–65

⚡ Lofty Spires

Between the end of the 14th century and the beginning of the 16th century, churches with lofty spires were built all over the region surrounding Salzburg: in Vigaun, Pfarrwerfen, Altenmarkt, St Veit, Bischofshofen, Hüttau, Mariapfarr, Felben near Mittersill and Maris Alm near Saalfelden.

mountain at close quarters, since you can drive directly up to the Arthurhaus (1,500 m/ 4,925 ft) by car, by bus or by taking the Hochkönig shuttle bus, which runs between Bischofshofen and Saalfelden. You can walk from here to the Mitterfeld-Alm (1,650m/ 5,420ft) in an hour. The ascent to the Matras-Haus (2,940m/9,640ft) on the Hochkönig should only be attempted by experienced, well-equipped walkers in good weather conditions (it takes a further five hours).

DIENTEN

Crossing the Dientener Sattel (1,360 m/4,450 ft) you will come to **Dienten am Hochköni**g (pop. 900; 23 km/14 miles).

The little parish church of **St Nicholas** (1506), with its baroque onion tower, is perched so picturesquely on a hill that its picture-postcard prettiness almost verges on the kitsch. The interior has the double nave typical of the churches of mining communities; collect the key from the priest's house to view the church.

Continuing over the Filzensattel (1,290 m/4,235 ft), you will shortly reach ★ **Maria Alm am Steinernen Meer** (pop. 2,000; 39 km/24 miles). The parish and pilgrimage church (1500–8) has the highest spire in Salzburg province; at 85 m (275 ft) it is even taller than that of Salzburg Cathedral.

Lichtenberg Castle

The elaborate baroque details were added during the 18th century. The portrait of the Virgin, to which are ascribed miraculous properties, is late Gothic (1480). The pilgrims in former times are said to have prayed to the portrait for relief from a plague of bears. Today, such assistance is no longer necessary; wild animals voluntarily keep at a safe distance since the area between Mühlbach and Saalfelden has developed into a skiers' paradise (160 km/100 miles of pistes, 200 km/125 miles of cross-country tracks). The big shots of politics and industry are particularly attracted to Maria Alm and the neighbouring skiing villages of **Hintermoos** and **Hinterthal**. Walking is possible at all times of the year. *(Information: Tourist Office, A-5761 Maria Alm, tel: 06584-7816.)*

SAALFELDEN

Saalfelden (pop. 12,600, 44 km/28 miles) lies in the Saalach Valley on the edge of the Zell Basin, framed by the Leoganger Steinberge and the Steinernes Meer on one side, and the Kitzbühel Alps and the Dienten Mountains on the other. Thanks to its favourable location, the area has been settled since prehistoric times. In more recent years the town became the administrative centre for the county of Unterpinzgau, and the seat of a number of aristocratic families.

Two devastating fires in 1734 and 1811 destroyed the old buildings. Worth visiting, however, is the **Pinzgau Museum of Local History** in Ritzen Castle (1604), which contains, along with other exhibits, the largest collection of Christmas cribs in Austria. Lake Ritzen's bathing beach is just one of the places where swimming is possible in summer. Still inhabited is the Rock Hermitage of St George (1664) above ★ **Lichtenberg Castle** (13th–19th century), northeast of Saalfelden. Children – and many adults – will be particularly interested in the longest summer toboggan run in Europe (1,600 m/1 mile). *(Information: Tourist Office, Bahnhofstrasse 10, A-5760 Saalfelden, tel: 06582-70660.)*

Star Attraction
• **Lichtenberg Castle**

Below: all set to ski
Bottom: logs chopped to burn

7: Mountain Road

Zell am See – Grossglockner Road – Heiligenblut (72 km/45 miles)

The Grossglockner Road *(see map below)* is in every respect the most dramatic of all the panoramic routes through the eastern Alps. Initial plans for a road across the Alps had been drawn up at the end of the 19th century, but it was not until after World War I that they actually became concrete. The prime aim of the road is not to fulfil a role in the national road network, but rather to serve touristic purposes. It was proposed to create an 'artificial road' which would become an attraction for holidaymakers. The commencement of the work was postponed several times for lack of funds, but the project finally went ahead in 1924 and was completed in 1935. Apart

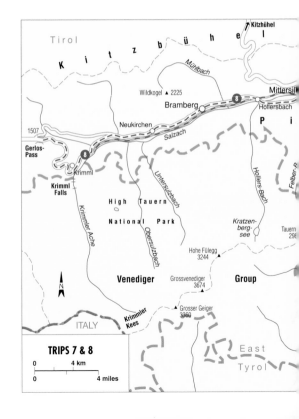

from the magnificent views, a notable attraction of the road is the fact that, in traversing it, one passes through a number of climatic zones, each with their corresponding types of vegetation. To the west and east of the road, the natural surroundings are strictly protected; the area forms part of the High Tauern National Park.

Today, each year, over 1 million visitors come to gaze down on to the Pasterze. This has provoked voices which claim that quotas must be set to limit the number of visitors in order to keep the environmental damage to a minimum. Those who wish to spare the mountains the toxic fumes of their own cars will choose to travel instead by the public bus which several times a day runs from Zell am See via Bruck up to the Franz-Josephs-Höhe and (by changing) on to Heiligenblut (and back).

> **High Tauern National Park**
>
> Information and maps are available from the tourist information offices of the communities within the park boundaries (Bad Gastein, Bramberg, Fusch, Hollersbach, Hüttschlag, Kaprun, Krimml, Mittersill, Mühr, Neukirchen, Rauris, Uttendorf and Wald). You can also apply to the National Park Administration, Franz-Josephs-Höhe, A-9844 Heiligenblut, tel: 04284-2727, or visit www.hohentauern.at.

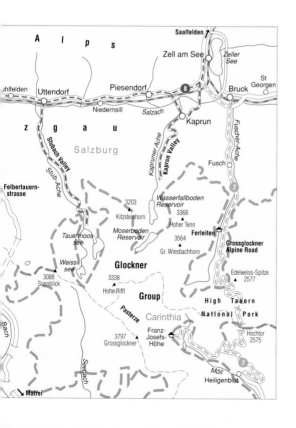

Map on pages 88–89

Bruck an der Grossglocknerstrasse

The ★★ **Grossglockner Road** starts in the centre of **Bruck an der Grossglocknerstrasse** (pop. 3,900). The **parish church** is neo-Gothic in style and was rebuilt following a fire in 1868–9. It contains a statue of the Virgin Mary which is believed to have miraculous properties and which, according to legend, mysteriously arrived in Bruck by floating down the Salzach on an ice floe. The pilgrims' invocation was 'Mary on the ice floe, protect us from danger as we go'. Note that the panoramic road remains closed to traffic because of adverse weather conditions from early November until the end of April. *(Information: Tourist Office, Glocknerstrasse 10, A-5671 Bruck, tel: 06546-7295.)*

The milestones along the panoramic section of the Grossglockner Road measure the distances from Bruck. The figures quoted in the following description match these distances. **Fusch an der Grossglocknerstrasse** (pop. 800; 7 km/4 miles) is the last village of any size before Heiligenblut. There used to be a second well-known village, Bad Fusch, until it burnt down in 1945. *(Information: Tourist Office, Grossglocknerstrasse 155, A-5672 Fusch, tel: 06546-236.)*

The Grossglockner Road continues along the course of the Fuscher Ache. The mountainous section begins near the Embach Chapel after 10 km (6 miles). Nowhere, however, does the gradient

Below: Bruck
Bottom: the mighty
Grosslockner

exceed 12 percent. After the Bärenschlucht, the Ferleiten, a lovely mountain pasture, opens up (1,145 m/3,756 ft; 14 km/9 miles). You can choose whether to stop at the National Park Information Office; at the toll booth, however, you have no choice. The charges are levied to pay for costly snow-clearing operations, maintenance of the road and environmental protection. The nature park at Ferleiten is home to a number of rare animals, including bears, wolves and lynxes.

Passing the Schleier Waterfall and the Piffalpe (1,400 m/4,600ft; 17 km/10 miles), you will arrive at the Piffkar (1,620 m/5,315 ft; 20 km/12 miles; carpark). This is the starting-point for the Piffkar panoramic footpath with information boards describing the local animal and plant life. The carpark at **Hochmais** (21 km/13 miles) affords perhaps the best view of the Grosses Wiesbachhorn (3,564 m/11,690 ft), the mountain with the highest precipice in the eastern Alps (see the nature information boards).

Star Attraction
• **Grossglockner Road**

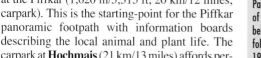

Elendboden Trail
When you reach the Elendboden (2,340 m/7,670 ft; 35 km/20 miles) there is a nature trail with display boards illustrating the geology of the Beindlkar National Park. The names serve as a reminder of the bones found here, which belonged to pilgrims who had died following an accident in 1683. In 1946 a pilgrim discovered a bronze dagger dating from the 17th century BC. Evidence of gold-mining activity in the area was also found.

THE HAIRPINS

After two more bends the road crosses a landslide area of dramatically jagged rocks with the appropriate name of Hexenküche (Witches' Kitchen) (2,060 m/6,750 ft; 23 km/14 miles). From the bridge on the valley side along the Edelweisswand (2,240 m/1,400 ft; 25 km/15 miles) you will be able to make out the remains of the so-called **Roman Road**; the latter is, however, a misnomer as the path was actually a trading and transport route for the gold mines dating from the Middle Ages.

At the Fuscher Törl (2,394 m/1,496 ft; 27 km/17 miles) there is a short side-road some 2 km (1 mile) long leading to the Edelweiss-Spitze (2,577 m/8,452 ft). It leads to the highest point along the route, from which you can enjoy a unique panorama of 37 mountain peaks, all more than 3,000 m (9,840 ft) high, and 19 glaciers. From this point the road continues downhill, past the Fuscher Lacke (2,260 m/7,420 ft; 30 km/20 miles), where you can see some further evidence of the 'Roman Road'. Carry on through the Mittertörl Tunnel, which is 120 m

A local resident

Map on pages 88–89

The Holy Blood

According to legend, in about 900 a Danish prince received some drops of the Holy Blood as a gift from the emperor of Byzantium, but died out in the snow at the foot of the Grossglockner on his way back to his native country. Three ears of corn growing out of the snow drew the attention of local peasants to the body and the precious relic, and they erected the first chapel of St Vincent on this spot.

(390 ft) long. During excavations for the Hochtor Tunnel the labourers discovered a clay lamp and a statue of Hercules, the Roman patron of mountain passes. In the middle of the tunnel you will cross the boundary to Carinthia. At the south end there is a car park with an observation point (2,500 m/ 8,210 ft; 30 km/20 miles).

In Guttal (1,860 m/6,100 ft; 40 km/25 miles) the road forks, and one arm, 8 km (5 miles), leads beside the glacier to the Franz-Josephs-Höhe. After 5 km (3 miles) you will reach the Glocknerhaus carpark; the traffic is controlled from this point as the car park on the Franz-Josephs-Höhe has a limited capacity. At the top you will find yourself facing the steep northern face of the ★★**Grossglockner** (3,800 m/12,454 ft), the tallest mountain in Austria which attracts over 1 million visitors a year. Looking down you will have a view of the **Pasterze Glacier**, which with an area of some 20 sq km (8 sq miles) is the largest in the eastern Alps.

HEILIGENBLUT

Heiligenblut

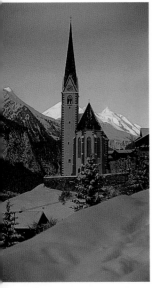

Passing the Kasereck (1,930 m/6,330 ft; 42 km/ 26 miles; car park with a view of the Grossglockner; remains of the 'Roman Road' on the mountain side) and the Mauthaus Heiligenblut (1,700 m/5,576 ft; 44 km/27 miles), you will finally arrive in ★ **Heiligenblut** (pop. 1,250; 1,300 m/4,267 ft; 49 km/30 miles), often described as the 'prettiest village in the Alps'. It is indeed a rarity to find an architectural jewel like the parish church of **St Vincent**, topped by a conspicuous spire, set against such a magnificent mountain panorama – a popular subject for postcards and calendars. The church was dedicated in 1491; the magnificent high altar was completed in 1520. It was the work of pupils of Michael Pacher, as can be seen from the similarities to the celebrated artist's altars in St Wolfgang and Gries (near Bolzano). The tabernacle rises up into the roof and contains the precious relic of the Holy Blood of Christ, which gave the village its name, and is the reason for which the church was originally built. (*Information: Tourist Association, A-9844 Heiligenblut, tel: 04824-2001–21.*)

8: Wintersport Wonderland

Zell am See – Kaprun Valley – Uttendorf – Stubach Valley – Mittersill – Neukirchen am Grossvenediger – Krimml – Gerlos Pass (72 km/ 45 miles)

This trip, a continuation of Trip 5 *(see pages 64–65)*, follows the Salzach back to its source along the edge of the High Tauern National Park. Detours into the side valleys of the Kaprun and Stubach will bring you closer to the beauties of nature and will introduce you to a number of technical achievements *(see map, pages 88–89)*.

A convenient alternative to using your own car is to take the Pinzgau Narrow-Gauge Railway, which follows the Saalach Valley from Zell am See to Krimml. If you want to explore the side valleys, however, you will need to change to the bus.

DETOUR INTO THE KAPRUN VALLEY

Kaprun (pop. 2,900), is the second most important centre of the European Sports Region after Zell am See. It offers facilities for 30 different sports disciplines on the ground, in the air and under water. In spite of the magnificence of the surrounding mountains, tourism is a relatively recent addition to the valley of the Kapruner

Map on pages 88–89

Star Attraction
• **Grossglockner**

Below: Edelweiss
Bottom: Kaprun

Map
on pages
88–89

Gentle Tourism

The communities within the national parks, which are all energetic supporters of the conservation concept, attempt to provide environmentally friendly alternatives to private transport. In the valleys, shuttle buses and taxis operate during the peak season; park rangers lead easy to moderate guided mountain walks and explain the plant and animal life and the geology and history of the region; there are also demonstrations of old craft techniques, folklore events, exhibitions and information evenings. Comfortable, well-run inns, *pensions* and farmhouses, together with a wide-ranging leisure program, encourage visitors to explore this beautiful countryside at a gentle pace.

*The Alpine Centre
at Kitsteinhorn Alps*

Ache. The boom began with the completion of a building project which usually detracts from the beauty of a valley: the Glockner-Kaprun power stations. The stream of visitors which began to arrive during the 1950s also encouraged the development of the Kitzsteinhorn (3200 m/10,500 ft) into an all-year skiing area.

LEISURE ACTIVITIES

In winter the Kaprun-Zell am See sports region includes 130 km (81 miles) of pistes and 300 km (188 miles) of cross-country tracks. Further amenities include the leisure centre (indoor and outdoor swimming pools, sauna). The **Mont Alpin** organises walks, climbing courses, etc. (*Information: Tourist Association, Salzburger Platz 601, A-5710 Kaprun, tel: 06547-8 6430.*)

Near the southern exit to the village on the right-hand side you will see the main power station (demonstration rooms open to the public daily). Shortly afterwards you will come to the valley station of the Maiskogel cable railway (830 m/2,720 ft). From the mountain station (1,550 m/5,085 ft; restaurant; footpaths) there is a fine panorama, which takes in the Grossglockner. Even better is the view from the Kitzsteinhorn (3,200 m/10,500 ft), which can be reached via cable cars from a number of points in the valley.

THE RESERVOIRS

Journey's end if you are travelling by private car or by bus is the Kesselfall House. A post bus runs from here to the Lärchenwand funicular. Once you reach the top, you can take the works shuttle bus along the Wasserfallboden Reservoir (1,680 m/5,375 ft) to the Moosboden Reservoir (2,040 m/6,690 ft; restaurants). This is a suitable starting-point for mountain tours of the surrounding peaks (only suitable for experienced climbers accompanied by a guide): the Grosses Wiesbachhorn (3,564 m/11,690 ft), the Hoher Tenn (3,368 m/11,047 ft) and the Hohes Riffl (3,338 m/10,949 ft). Depending on the weather situation, trips up to the mountain reservoirs can be made daily between late May and early October.

Below: view from the Kittzsteinhorn
Bottom: an Alpine welcome

UTTENDORF

The words 'power plant' and 'weir' have become bones of contention ever since economic necessity and increasing concern about the conservation of nature began to clash with each other. But looking across the two Tauern power-station reservoirs may help to make you forget some of your prejudices. Despite the massive remodelling of the landscape you will be enchanted by the view. The first discussions concerning this project, which was to become a watchword for Austrian development after the two world wars, were actually held in 1929. In 1944 the main power station in Kaprun with the auxiliary Wasserfallboden reservoir was commissioned. Eight years later, the power station linked to the Mooserboden and Margaritze were added. In 1955 the upper section with the Wasserfallboden reservoir was completed.

Uttendorf (pop. 2,800; 20 km/12 miles). This little village, adorned by a late Gothic parish church and the Gothic church of **St Margaret** (with a Romanesque core and frescoes) is the starting-point for a side trip into the **Stubach Valley**, which is 17 km (11 miles) long and framed by mountains forming part of the **High Tauern National Park** *(see page 96)*. For infor-

Map on pages 88–89

mation, contact the office at the bathing beach. (Bus from Uttenberg cable railway station on the Enzinger Boden.)

Detour into the Stubach Valley

With its picturesque countryside, the Stubach Valley was the starting-point for the idea of a High Tauern National Park, first proposed at the beginning of this century. During the 1970s, however, it was already too late to integrate the valley into the protected area, since the energy industry had already made its presence felt by this stage. What remained, however, was the Wiegenwald, a forest of stone pines dotted with moorland lakes; untouched for centuries. This unspoilt biotope may be entered only in the company of a guide (*information and applications: Uttendorf Tourist Office, Dorfbachstrasse 27a; tel: 06563-82790*).

Below: Mittersill Castle
Bottom: Stubach Valley

From the Enzinger Boden (1,470 m/4,815 ft) and the power station of the same name you can ascend by cable car to the **Rudolfshütte** (2,310 m/7,577 ft), owned by the Austrian Alpine Society (tel: 06563-8221). Here you will find not only a hotel and restaurant but also an alpine training centre and a base for ski and mountain touring. Two glacier nature trails begin here: one leads along the south shore of the Weissee (2,250 m/7,380 ft) and on to the Stubacher Sonnblick-Kees (2,500 m/8,200 ft; 3 hours), whilst the other heads towards the Eisbodenlacke (2,070 m/6,790 ft) and the Ödenwinkel-Kees (2,150 m/7,050 ft; 3 hours). If you want to climb higher still, you should take the Medelzkopf cable car to the mountain station at 2,550 m (8,365 ft).

Mittersill

Returning to the Salzach, the next ports of call along your route will be **Stuhlfelden** (25 km/ 15 miles), which boasts a Romanesque **Church of the Assumption** with Gothic vaulting, choir and west tower, and **Mittersill** (pop. 5,400, 28 km/18 miles). Since medieval times the principal town of the Pinzgau has stood at the crossroads of two important routes. Almost all its medieval buildings were destroyed by fire; among the oldest remaining buildings are **Mittersill Castle** (16th century), the parish church of St Leonard (1747–9) and the church of St Anne (1751).

In the suburb of Felben, a pleasing ensemble is formed by the **late-Gothic church** of St Nicholas, which has a Romanesque core, the **Felber Tower** (12th-century residence of the rulers of Felben) and the surrounding farmhouses. The **Museum of Local History** is housed in the dramatic Felber Tower and in the Pinzgau Farmhouse. *(Information: Tourist Office, Marktplatz 4, A-5730 Mittersill, tel: 06562-4292.)*

THE FELBERTAUERN ROAD

Mittersill also marks the beginning of the Felbertauern Road leading towards East Tyrol. This panoramic road provides a particularly scenic north-south link through the Austrian Alps.

Neukirchen am Grossvenediger (pop. 2,500; 45 km/28 miles) lies clustered at the foot of **Hohenneukirchen Castle** (13th century with more recent additions; today an old people's

The Tauern Cycle Path
The Tauern Cycle Path, which is clearly marked along its entire length, leads along 300km (190 miles) of cycle-tracks and quiet roads through a wide variety of landscapes. It winds through the Krimml Waterfalls in the High Tauern National Park to the Pongau and the Tennengau on to Salzburg, continuing through the gently undulating countryside of the Alpine foothills to Passau and beyond. The route follows the downhill course of the Salzach, so there are no uphill sections.

Two wheels good on the Felbertauern Road

Map
on pages
88–89

*Below: the castle at Hohenneukirchen
Bottom: hats for sale at Grossvenediger*

home), surrounding the massive tower of the **parish church**, which has a Gothic exterior and baroque interior. The village has been awarded a number of prizes for its appearance and environmental consciousness. *(Information: Tourist Office, Marktstrasse 171, A-5741 Neukirchen am Grossvenediger, tel: 06565-62560.)*

THE GROSSVENEDIGER

In spite of its impressive title, Neukirchen is still some way from the majestic ★★ **Grossvenediger**. At the Hopffelboden carpark in the Obersulzbach Valley begins a two- to three-day tour (for experienced climbers only) via the Berndlalm (1,515 m/4,970 ft), past a glacier nature trail, across the Postalm to the Kürsinger Hütte (6 hours). If you can muster the energy, carry on for a further 4 hours and you will reach the summit of the Grossvenediger (3,675 m/12,055 ft). A shorter, less exhausting excursion is to take the **Wildkogel cable car** from Neukirchen to the Braunkogel (2,167 m/7,108 ft), where there is a **mountain restaurant** and the **Wildkogel skiing area**.

KRIMML

Krimml (pop. 900; 58 km/36 miles), the site of the ★★ **Krimml Waterfalls**, provides the highlight of Trip 8. The Ache cascades a spectacular total of 380 m (1,264 ft) over three rock sills down into the Salzach and are among the highest in Europe. A footpath leads beside the watercourse, which is bordered by beautiful forests. The views are breathtaking and it is worth building in some time into your schedule to enjoy this area. There are observation platforms that are situated so close to the spray that you are surrounded by a watery mist – a magnificent natural phenomenon.

A WALK UP THE FALLS

For the average walker, the walk from the car park near the waterfalls to above the third and highest sill will take approximately 2 hours. If you are an experienced walker you can continue for another hour through the valley of the Krimmler Ache to the Krimmler Tauernhaus (1,620 m/5,320 ft; with restaurant), or even further on to the end of the valley at the edge of the glacier of the Krimmler Kees (2,000 m/6,500 ft; another 2½ hours). Here you are unlikely to encounter many other walkers, which can hardly be said of the waterfalls themselves: during the peak season, thousands of visitors throng to this spot to see the thundering spectacle. *(Information: Tourist Office, Oberkrimml 37, A-5743 Krimml, tel: 06564-7239.)*

Star Attraction
• **Krimml Waterfalls**

THE GERLOS PASS ROAD

On the road out of Krimml lies the toll station for the **Gerlos Pass**, which leads through the mountainous Kitzbühel Alps. After a number of bends you will skirt the **Gerlosplatte**, a favourite ski region (Hochkrimml-Gerlosplatte). The source of the Salzach lies in the skiing region of **Almdorf-Königsleiten** to the north. Beside the Durlassboden Reservoir on the far side of the Gerlos Pass (1,510 m/4,930 ft), where there are facilities for sailing, you will cross the border into the neighbouring province of Tyrol (72 km/45 miles).

> **Krimml in Winter**
> The Krimml waterfalls are not only spectacular in summer. In winter, they turn into a huge 'ice-fall'. Although the falls are officially closed in winter, it is possible to view them from the bottom. There is no charge for entry in the winter.

Krimml Waterfalls

Art History

Salzburg's perpetual charm lies in the gradually evolving harmony between architecture and landscape. The region was settled from earliest times, but the real beginning of Salzburg's documented history can be traced back to St Rupert. In about AD 700 the Bishop of Worms chose the village as the centre for his missionary campaign; in those days, there was probably just a small monastery of monks here, living amidst the ruins of the Roman town of *Iuvavum*. St Rupert reorganised the Monastery of St Peter and founded its church as well as the convent on the Nonnberg. A century later, Salzburg was elected an archbishopric, thus becoming the provincial religious centre with a sphere of influence which at certain times reached as far as Hungary.

The town and the surrounding region were greatly influenced by the archbishops, who during the baroque era ruled with the might of absolute monarchs. Archbishop Wolf Dietrich von Raitenau, a relative of the Medici family, ascended the archbishop's throne in 1587 and began to transform the little medieval town into a magnificent baroque princely residential city along Italian lines. Entire districts of the town, then a maze of narrow, twisting alleys bordered by narrow houses like those still standing in the Judengasse and Steingasse today, were demolished to make way for spacious squares with sumptuous palaces. Wolf Dietrich's successors and their architects continued with the rebuilding of the town, achieving a graceful harmony between buildings, squares and streets.

Under the regency of the prince-bishops the ordinary citizens had little influence on political and cultural developments. This is clear from the modest proportions of the town hall.

ART AND ARCHITECTURE

During the **Celtic era** (450–15 BC), it was customary to place jewellery, weapons, drinking vessels and other items in the graves of the dead, a

---

What's in a name?
The heart of the Old City is crossed by the River Salzach, along which the boatmen used to transport the valuable salt from Hallein and Reichenhall. This helps to explains the name of the city: the landmark Salzachburg – the Fortress on the Salzach – is visible from afar to this day, and became known in time as Salzburg.

Opposite: musical interlude at Hellbrunn Palace
Below: stones along the Roman road

Celtic treasures
For a more comprehensive insight into the Celtic era visit the Celtic Museum in Hallein as well as the open-air sites on the Dürrnberg *(see page 63)* which includes a reconstruction of a Celtic farmstead complex and grave.

Roman mosaic

tradition that has preseved the beauty of form and the mysterious fascination of the motifs used in Celtic artefacts. One of the most important examples is the bronze beaked can now on view in the **Carolino Augusteum Museum** in Salzburg *(see page 35)*, which was discovered on the Dürrnberg near Hallein, one of the most significant sites for the discovery of Celtic treasures.

The relics of the **Roman era** in Salzburg (15 BC–5th century AD) include, among other things, some fine mosaic floors. They are also on display in museums, including the Carolino Augusteum Museum. The Roman occupation of the area was concentrated on the city of Salzburg itself, or *Iuvavum*. Along the former Imperial Roman Road, which largely followed the route of today's B99 across the Radstädter Tauern, you will spot at intervals Roman milestones and votive stones. Relief gravestones set into the walls (for instance, those of the parish churches of St Michael and St Martin) point to the fact that there was once a Roman staging post in the Lungau.

The conversion of the eastern Alpine region to Christianity under St Rupert and the missionary activity centred on the Monastery of St Peter gave rise to a period of intense building activity after AD 696. By the end of the 8th century the archbishopric of Salzburg was already in possession of 67 churches and 11 monasteries. Archaeological excavations, however, have failed to reveal more than the remains of a handful of buildings, most of them the predecessors of modern complexes.

Few individual objects remain from the Early Middle Ages: the large Cross of St Rupert in the parish church at Bischofshofen, covered with embossed gilt copper sheeting and decorated with glass gems, is thought to have been brought to Salzburg from Northumbria under Bishop Virgil. Scholars are certain, however, that another medieval treasure, a precious manuscript, was actually produced in Salzburg. During the last quarter of the 8th century Cuthbert, a monk from the British Isles, produced in the scriptorium in Salzburg the masterpiece which later came to be named after him: the *Cutbercht Evangelium* (today in the Austrian National Library in Vienna). The miniatures with which he illuminated his work reveal the influence of the British Isles and Northern Italy. Following Charlemagne's victory over Duke Tassilo of Bavaria in 788 and the integration of the latter's territory into his empire, the influence of Carolingian courtly art made its presence felt in the scriptorium in Salzburg.

With the development of the **Romanesque** style in the 11th–12th century the bookmaker's art experienced another Golden Age in Salzburg. Through contacts with Venice, the monks learned to appreciate Byzantine art; contacts were established with the important centres of south and west Germany, including Regensburg. A number of outstanding works were produced between 1050 and 1150: the *Pericope of Custos Perhtold* (today in New York), the *Antiphonal of St Peter* (today in Vienna) and the *Walther Bible* (produced on the orders of Abbot Walther of Michaelbeuern and still on view in the monastery library there; *see page 48*).

Between the covers of these books you will find paintings in brilliant colours bearing vivid witness to the artistic skills of an era. Panel painting did not really begin to develop until the 13th century, and wall paintings were almost always destroyed by later building projects or the passage of time. For this reason the frescoes dating from about 1140 in the convent church of the Benedictine nuns on the

Below: Nonnberg Convent
Bottom: Monastery of St Peter

Below: altar in the Franciscan Church
Bottom: cemetery at the Monastery of St Peter

Nonnberg have a certain scarcity value. Significant remains of late Romanesque frescoes have also survived in the parish churches of some of the villages in the Lungau: Mariapfarr (*c*1220) and Weisspriach (*c*1200 and 1250), as well as in the unadorned Church of St George in Bischofshofen (*c*1230). The nave of the Franciscan Church in Salzburg itself is an example of a Romanesque sacred building; other examples can be discerned only in part, due to later rebuilding, or exist only in the general overall shape (the Abbey Church of St Peter in Salzburg, and churches in Lamprechtshausen, Mariapfarr, Zell am See, Stuhlfelden, Grödig, Michaelbeuern and Mattsee). More easily recognisable, by contrast, are the Romanesque elements of the castles: the fortresses of Hohensalzburg and Hohenwerden were begun in 1077, Mauterndorf Castle was built in about 1250 and Moosham Castle soon afterwards.

The **Gothic era** left its mark on the city's countenance, an influence which can still be seen today. The oldest memorial to this period is the Chapel of St Mary in St Peter's Monastery, which was rebuilt in 1319. The Spital Church, today the Church of St Blasius, is the earliest example of a hall church (in which the nave and the aisles are of equal height) in South Germany and West Austria; it was built between 1327–50. In 1460 came the dedication of the magnificent hall choir of the Franciscan

Church, planned in 1408 by the famous architect Hans von Burghausen.

In the period between the end of the 14th and the beginning of the 16th century, churches with lofty spires were built all over the region surrounding Salzburg: in Vigaun, Pfarrwerfen, Altenmarkt, St Veit, Bischofshofen, Hüttau, Mariapfarr, Felben near Mittersill and Maria Alm near Saalfelden. Some of them, as for example in Kuchl, Dienten, Irrsdorf, Lofer and Torren near Golling, were later adorned with a baroque cupola. St Leonard's Church at Tamsweg is a remarkable jewel of Late Gothic architecture, which not only enjoys a delightful situation but has also retained its original glass windows. In marked contrast, the most important wood carver and artist of the Late Gothic era, Michael Pacher, created works of stark realism and dynamic composition. He completed his principal work, the altar in St Wolfgang, in 1481. Of his altar for the Franciscan Church in Salzburg (where he died in 1498), only the figure of the Virgin Mary with the Infant Christ remains as the centrepiece of Johann Bernhard Fischer von Erlach's baroque high altar.

The **Italian Renaissance** reached Salzburg relatively late, which seems surprising in view of the geographical proximity and the close economic contacts with northern Italy. The political upheavals of the time probably hindered the commissioning of works of art and large building projects. The arcaded courtyard of the Spital in Salzburg (1556–62) is one of the few surviving examples of Renaissance architecture in a city in which that style was rarely seen. The marble altar (1518) in St Georgen in the Pinzgau and the frescoes of the Knights' Hall in Goldegg Castle (1536) are notable examples to be found in the surrounding region.

Archbishop Wolf Dietrich von Raitenau (1587–1612), a relative of the Milan branch of the Medici family, initiated a period of lively building activity with the aim of transforming medieval Salzburg into a princely capital along Italian lines. He bought up an entire section of the city to provide sufficient space for the generous proportions of a number of squares: the Residenzplatz,

> **The 'Gentle' manner**
> In some Late Gothic churches (for example Altenmarkt or in the abbey Church of St Peter in Salzburg) you will still find a 'Lovely Madonna' created in the 'International' or 'Gentle' manner. This was a style which spread across Central Europe from Bohemia in about 1400, characterised by soft, flowing forms and sweet faces. Salzburg became one of the most important centres for this trend.

Neptune's Fountain at Kapitelplatz

Below: the Horse Fountain
Bottom: Mozart's house

Mozartplatz, Kapitelplatz and Domplatz. The construction of the Chapter House, the New Building and the Residence in the style of magnificent *palazzi* began; in 1606 the archbishop also took on the court stable. Following the fire of 1598 he had the cathedral demolished completely and commissioned a new building. The first plans were the work of Vincenzo Scamozzi; in 1614, Santino Solari produced a new design and supervised its execution. The new cathedral was modelled on the style of the Jesuit church, Il Gesù, in Rome and later became in its turn the model for many churches in the South German area. On the outskirts of town Altenau Palace, the predecessor of Mirabell Palace, was built for Wolf Dietrich's mistress Salome Alt and their children. The interior design of St Gabriel's Chapel focuses on Wolf Dietrich's own unique mausoleum, lying at the centre of the Cemetery of St Sebastian, which is surrounded by arcades in the style of a Campo Santo.

Wolf Dietrich's successors, including Marcus Sitticus von Hohenems (1612–9) and Paris Lodron (1619–53), continued his building schemes in the Italian style; the most attractive example is Hellbrunn Palace, a *villa suburbana* to the south of the princely capital.

The transformation of the city's countenance reached its zenith during the **high and late baroque** eras, initially under the supervision of

Italian architects. Giovanni Antonio Dario built Maria Plain (1671–4) while Johann Caspar Zucchali built St Erhard (1685–9) and the Church of St Cajetan (1685–97). Archbishop Johann Ernst Thun (1687–1709), however, preferred local artists, in particular Johann Bernhard Fischer von Erlach. The latter was responsible for the Winter Riding School built into the rock face of the Mönchsberg, the facade and drinking trough of the court stables, the Church of the Holy Trinity, the Collegiate Church, the St John's Spital Church and the former Ursuline Church (now St Mark's), as well as Klessheim Palace and the pilgrimage church of Maria Kirchenthal near Lofer. Johann Lukas von Hildebrandt was responsible for the design of Mirabell Palace.

In addition to the work of these two great masters of Austrian baroque architecture, Salzburg also benefited from the activities of some of the country's most celebrated artists, such as Martino Altomonte, Paul Troger and Johann Michael Rottmayr. Many of Austria's greatest sculptors were also at work in Salzburg during this period. Bernhard Michael Mandl, for example, created the equestrian group for the drinking trough of the court stables (Horse Trough) while Meinrad Guggenbichler produced a number of fine altars.

The early **Classical era** in Salzburg, most clearly demonstrated by the work of the brothers Wolfgang and Johann Baptist Hagenauer (responsible for the New Gate and St Mary's Column in Salzburg, churches in Hallein and Böckstein and the high altar in Köstendorf), was followed by the secularisation of the rule of the prince-bishops. This period was a time of stagnation and decline in the fields of art and building. Many of the secular rulers appropriated for themselves most of the moveable works of art in the former archbishops' collections in their residences. As a consequence, Salzburg lost a large proportion of its cultural heritage.

The **Romantic era** bequeathed to the Salzburg area two interesting examples of characteristic architecture: Anif Castle, inspired by the English Gothic style (1838–48), and the neo-Gothic Pongau Cathedral in St Johann (1855–61). During

> **Meinrad Guggenbichler**
> You will find a number of altars produced by Meinrad Guggenbichler and his atelier at Mondsee, not only in the former princely capital, but dotted throughout the entire province of Salzburg and in the Salzkammergut. His masterpieces are generally considered to be the altars in the parish churches of Mondsee and St Wolfgang; others examples can be found in the churches in Michaelbeuern, Strasswalchen and Irrsdorf.

A stroll through Hellbrunn Palace

this period painters such as G F Waldmüller, F Gauermann and Rudolf von Alt discovered the Salzkammergut as a source of themes for their landscape paintings. Vienna was, however, the centre of artistic activity, where Hans Makart, a native son of Salzburg, determined the style and taste of high society.

Below: sculpture at the Museum of Modern Art
Bottom: the Festival Halls

Anton Faistauer, born in St Martin near Lofer and one of the most important artists of the inter-war years, retained his close links with Salzburg although he lived in Vienna. He belonged to a group of painters whose primarily colourist style diverged from the academic tendency of the historicist school and the formalism of art nouveau. Faistauer was responsible for the magnificent frescoes decorating the foyer of the Small Festival Playhouse.

The standard of **20th-century architecture** in Salzburg ranges from the sensitive solutions of the Festival Playhouses (1926–39 and 1956–60) by Clemens Holzmeister, which blend harmoniously with the historical setting, and notoriously insensitive ones such as the former Café Winkler (Cziharz/Lenk, 1975–6).

From the 1950s onwards, the architectural crimes perpetrated in the Old Town and the surrounding area assumed alarming proportions. When the 1967 conservation law governing the preservation of the Old Town failed to bring the mushrooming of contemporary buildings under

control, a citizens' action group took over. Following the landslide victory of the Citizens' List in the local elections of 1983, a Planning Committee was founded. This panel of experts now has the task of assessing plans for all new buildings and for the conversion of existing ones before any construction work commences.

Had it not been for energetic private initiative, the city of Salzburg would have little to show when it came to the **Fine Arts of the 20th century**. The efforts of private citizens led to the opening of the gallery in the Residence as a gallery of local art in 1923. The Salzburg Museum of Baroque Art, opened in 1973, was based on the private collection of Kurt Rossacher. In 1954, the art dealer Friedrich Welz, in association with Oskar Kokoschka, initiated the International Summer Academy of Fine Arts in the Fortress of Hohensalzburg, which has been held on an annual basis ever since. In 1976, through his donation of a wideranging collection of modern art (including Gustav Klimt and Oskar Kokoschka), Welz laid the foundation for the Salzburg Provincial Collection, the Rupertinum. Since 1983 the group of paintings have been housed in the former Collegium, which dates from the 17th century.

Lack of space at the Carolino Augusteum Museum gave birth to the idea of an art gallery on the Mönchsberg. The collection was moved to its new location in the Modern Art Gallery in 2004. The Carolino Augusteum is moving to the Residenz building in 2006.

The Festival City

When the age of spiritual rulers drew to a close in 1803 and the former princely capital was absorbed into the Archduchy of Austria in 1816, a certain creative vacuum arose. In the mid-19th century, however, Salzburg found a new identity through its most famous son, Wolfgang Amadeus Mozart (1756–91). The centenary celebrations of Mozart's birth in 1856 were held in honour of a composer who had once been literally kicked out of the service of the Prince-Bishop Hieronymus Colloredo,

Sound of Music film locations

To US and British audiences, Salzburg's most famous film is *The Sound of Music*. Much of the film was made on location in and around the city and today, scores of fans still flock to retrace the Trapp family's steps. Among the locations used in the film were: the Mirabell Gardens where '*Do Re Mi*' was sung around the fountain. St Peter's Cemetery was reconstructed in the studios and used for the scene where the Trapp family hide between the tombstones when trying to escape detection by the Nazis. The façade of Fohnburg Castle was used as the front of the Trapp villa while Leoploldskron Castle was used as the rear of the villa. The children go boating on the lake there and the ballroom was modelled on one of the rooms inside. The opening scenes in the convent were filmed at Nonnberg Abbey; the famous opening credit scenes were filmed around Lake Fuschl and the wedding at the church in Mondsee. The Trapp family make their escape over the Untersberg (in reality, this would not have been a wise move as it would have taken them straight to the location of Hitler's Eagle's Nest) and many other snippets of the city are used as backdrops throughout the film.

Max Reinhardt (1873–1943)

Max Reinhardt was one of the co-founders of the Salzburg Festival. Born in Baden near Vienna in 1873, he was forced into exile in the USA in 1938. He was also the founder of the Max Reinhardt Seminar at the University of Vienna. This is a drama college, which continues to run four-year acting courses.

The Mozart family grave

and who 'cared very little for Salzburg' (to use one of his less colourful expressions). The Cathedral Music Association and Mozarteum had been founded as early as 1841. This body was later to evolve into the International Mozarteum Foundation, devoted to the furthering of and research into Mozart's music, along with the Mozarteum Academy of Music and Dramatic Art. During the following decades, a succession of large-scale musical celebrations was held in Salzburg.

A spark of genius was supplied by the theatre producer Max Reinhardt, who came up with the idea of a Salzburg Festival. 'Here, where the eye delights everywhere it looks, where every glimpse encounters exquisite harmony, where an entire city reveals beauty in its innermost being; here is the right place to celebrate a festival,' he pronounced. In 1917 he presented his plans for the organisation of a festival as well as the erection of a festival hall. The same year saw the founding of the Salzburg Festival Community. On its artistic committee sat leading artists of the time: Max Reinhardt, the conductor Franz Schalk, the composer Richard Strauss, the poet Hugo von Hofmannsthal and the set-designer Alfred Roller. In spite of financial difficulties and planning problems, particularly after the collapse of the Danube monarchy in 1918, the festival opened in 1920 with Hofmannsthal's *Jedermann* (Everyman) under the direction of Max Reinhardt. The actors performed without fees, with the exception of Werner Krauss, who played Death and the Devil; he insisted on payment in the form of a pair of Salzburg *Lederhosen*. The mystery play of the life and death of a rich man, performed in front of the perfect setting of the west front of the cathedral, rapidly gained in popularity and became an essential part of the festival.

In 1922, Hofmannsthal's *Great Salzburg World Theatre* received its premiere in the Collegiate Church. In addition, an opera was performed for the first time in the Regional Theatre: Mozart's *Don Giovanni*. In the same year the foundation stone was laid for the Festival Hall in Hellbrunn Park, but unfortunately there was no money to complete the project. In 1924, it was decided to use part of the princely stables for the project. Over the decades, this makeshift solution was extended by the addition of new buildings and reconstruction of old ones to create today's festival complex. Closely linked with the name of the architect, Clemens Holzmeister, the Small and Large Festival Halls and the open-air stage of the Summer Riding School (built directly into the mountainside) extend behind the long facade of the former princely stables.

The festival completely transformed Salzburg during the 1920s. The little town which Stefan Zweig had chosen to live in 'above all because of its romantic remoteness' became during the course of just a few years one of the great cultural centres of Europe. 'I have many happy memories of the Salzburg of the late 1920s and early 1930s, when it was a mecca for many artists, a unique blend of the spirit of Mozart and the most modern and daring trends in music, art, theatre and stage design,' reminisced Robert Stolz. The festival's typical style of performance was determined above all by Max Reinhardt, Bruno Walter and Arturo Toscanini. The *Anschluss* of Austria with the German Reich in 1938 put an end to the work of these and many other artists, when the Salzburg Festival was appropriated by the Nazi propaganda machine.

During the postwar years, the names of other great artists were associated with outstanding per-

Below: a performance of Jedermann
Bottom: the Advent Concert

formances. In 1960 Herbert von Karajan opened the Large Festival Hall with the *Rosenkavalier* by Richard Strauss and Hugo von Hofmannsthal. Until his death in 1989, Karajan's influence decisively shaped the festival. The post-Karajan era, under the direction of Hans Landesmann, Gerard Mortier, Heinrich Wiesmüller and the actor Peter Stein, opened in 1991 with a play: Shakespeare's *Julius Caesar*.

The festival, which is now enveloped in a network of other cultural activities spread across the whole year, is a major attraction and an important economic factor for the city. But the city's cultural highlights are not set by the festival alone: top orchestras and international musicians perform within the framework of the *Mozart Week* (end of January). The *Easter Festival*, founded by Herbert von Karajan in 1967, consists of two performance cycles, each including an opera, an oratorio and two orchestral concerts. Also founded by Herbert von Karajan, the annual *Whitsun Concerts* feature different world-class orchestras.

Since 1954 there have also been the *Castle Concerts*, the 'greatest chamber music series in the world', which run throughout the year in the Marble Hall of Mirabell Palace and in the Knights' Hall of the Residence. Even the *Hohensalzburg Concerts* (March to October) owe part of their success to the atmosphere of the room in which they

Below:plaque at Mozart's birthplace
Bottom: the auditorium at the Festival Halls

MOZARTS GEBVRTSHAVS
MOZART-MVSEVM
IN DIESEM HAVSE WVRDE
W. A. M O Z A R T A M
27.JANNER 1756 GEBOREN

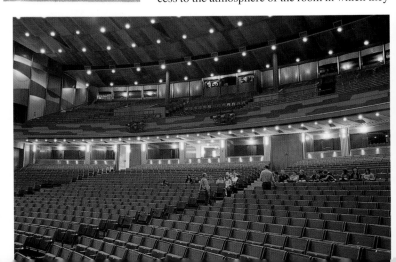

are performed. The *Salzburg Operetta Concerts* (May–October) are performed in the Chapter Room. The *Mozart Serenades* (April–October) are performed in historic costumes. The *Residence Mozart Matinées* are midday concerts in the New Building of the Residence (July to September).

The *Scene* has established itself since 1971 as an avant-garde festival (July). In the first two weekends of August there is the *Festival in Hellbrunn*, with opera, theatre, music and dance in the palace and at different venues in the park. There are also musical events later in the year. The cultural highlight in autumn is the *Culture Days* (October). Pre-Christmas concerts complete the Festival year, including the famous *Advent Concert*, held in the Large Festival Hall.

Theatres, Concerts and Folklore

Landestheater (Salzburg Regional Theatre), Schwarzstrasse 22 and 24, tel: 8715120; www.theater.co.at. Opera, plays, ballet.

Marionettentheater, Schwarzstrasse 24, tel: 8724060; fax: 882141; www.marionetten.at. Austria's most famous puppet theatres perform operas.

Puppentheater 'Le Parapluie', Itzlinger Hauptstrasse 37, tel: 53574; fax: 452439. Puppet theatre.

TOI-Haus, Theater and Mirabellplatz, Hubert-Sattler-Gasse 3, tel: 874439. Theatre for the young.

Komödie Salzburg, Itzlinger Hauptstrasse 37, tel: 53574; fax: 452439. Boulevard theatre.

Hohensalzburg concerts (in the Princes' Room): Anton-Adlgasser-Weg 22, tel: 825858; fax: 825859.

Mozart Serenades (in the Gothic Hall of the Civic Hospital, in Hellbrunn Palace and in the Mozarteum): Mozarteum Foundation, Postfach 34, tel: 873154; fax: 872996.

The Sound of Music Dinner Show, Sternbräu; www.soundof musicshow.com. Daily April to October.

Festival Halls, Hofstallgasse; tel: 840997; fax: 847835.

Operetta concerts (performed in the Chapter Hall), tel: 845-571256/662109.

Ticket Offices in Salzburg

Polzer: Residenzplatz 3, tel: 846500.

Kultur: Büro, Linzergasse 14, tel: 870480.

Hellbrunn Festival: Postfach 47, 5027 Salzburg, tel: 878784.

Easter Festival: Herbert von Karajan Platz 9, tel: 8045361; www.oster-festspiele-salzburg.at

Salzburg Festival and Whitsun Festival: Postfach 140, Hofstallgasse 1, tel: 8045500; www.salzburgfestival.at

Republic (avant-garde theatre and dance festival): Anton-Neumayr-Platz 2, tel: 843448, fax: 846808.

Try also the Ticket Shop, Getreidegasse 5, tel: 847767, fax: 849769; www.salzburg.co.at/ticket.shop.

Landestheater poster

FOOD AND DRINK

The Cuisine of Salzburg

Does Salzburg actually possess a cuisine of its own? Apart from the *Salzburger Nockerl* (soufflé omelette), no other Salzburg speciality springs to mind. Even experts do not claim that the town is responsible for any other characteristic dishes, a situation which they blame on the city's historical background as the residence of the prince-bishops. The court was a meeting-place of international diplomacy and Salzburg itself a crossroads of international trading routes. This meant that local chefs were subject to a wide variety of external influences, which tended to hinder the development of a local cuisine in the city.

On the other hand, the princely capital was always the seat of refined culinary skills. To be more precise, the court of the prince-archbishop was a gourmet's paradise. In 1719 a *New Salzburg Cookery Book* was published, comprised of recipes collected by the court chef, Conrad Hager. But the local populace could not try out the fine dishes with their expensive ingredients, and regulations prohibited culinary luxury for the ordinary people of the town.

Today, the cuisine of Vienna dominates Austria, having succeeded in adapting to its own use the best recipes from all the countries of the Habsburg empire, especially those from Bohemia and Hungary. And yet it is this inimitable blend which has enabled it to shine in its own right.

If you study more closely the menus displayed in restaurants in town and country, you will notice certain preferences which one could certainly regard as typical of Salzburg. You will find a large number of dishes employing cheese, *Kasnocken* (home-made cheese noodles) for example, or *Kassuppe* (cheese soup), testifying to the importance of the dairy industry in the region. And if you take a look into the cooking pots of the area's rural population, as a number of famous restaurant owners and chefs have already done, you will find a number of other delicious cheese recipes, for example *Stinkerknödel*, which is made with potatoes and cheese. Sauerkraut is an important accompaniment: *Krautspatz* are noodles with sauerkraut and *Hoargneistnidei* is the unpronounceable name for a loaf made of baked sauerkraut.

Austria's baked puddings are a dangerous temptation for all visitors with a sweet tooth. The term *Mehlspeisen* includes most sweet puddings, even if they do not contain flour. The choice includes gâteaux and tarts, cakes and strudel, apricot and plum dumplings (made with potato dough), stuffed pancakes and *Kaiserschmarrn*, a kind of sliced pancake. Salzburg's main contribution in this sphere is the *Salzburger Nockerln*, which are 'as sweet as love and as delicate as a kiss', and highly sensitive to draughts. The main ingredient is stiffly beaten egg whites, which means they are a sort of sweet soufflé. The Salzburg region has developed a series of individual recipes for the batter for *Strauben*, a type of doughnut. The best ones of all are made with choux pastry, deep-fried and dusted with icing sugar and cinnamon.

A stroll through the centre of Salzburg will make it clear which alcoholic drink Salzburg has adopted as its own. Stern-Bräu, Stiegl-Bräu-Keller, Augustiner-Bräu-Stübl and other tavern signs make it only too obvious: Salzburg is a beer town – with the attractive side-effects of numerous inns and beer gardens. You can order a *grosses Bier* (½ litre) or a *kleines* (⅓ litre) from these places, which also offer a selection of good food.

Salzburg has no wine-growing area of its own. The wines on offer on city menus are usually from Lower Austria, the Burgenland or South Tyrol. A *Gspritzer* is wine with the addition of mineral water.

Salzburg's cafes are an institution. It is likely that the famous festival would not exist were it not for the Tomaselli, the Mozart, the Glockenspiel or the Bazar, where artists and men of letters used to meet, especially before World War II. Today the atmospheric cafés are often full to bursting point. You should not, however, simply order a coffee with your cake. Austria has countless ways of preparing coffee which are named according to the size of the 'dish' in which they are served and the ratio of coffee to milk. A *Kleiner Brauner* is served in a mocca cup, a *Grosser Brauner* in a double mocca cup. A *Kurzer* is a strong espresso, a *Verlängerter* a weak one. *Melange* is coffee with milk and whipped cream, *Einspänner* a double mocca in a tall glass with plenty of whipped cream. Many other coffee specialities include a shot of alcohol.

RESTAURANTS AND TAVERNS
Taverns

Augustinerbräu, Augustinergasse 4, tel: 431246. Old monastery that has been brewing its own beer for hundreds of years. Wonderful beer garden in summer (bring your own picnic or choose from the various stalls). €

Gablerbräu, Linzergasse 9, tel: 88965. Old brewery with good, plain Austrian food. €€

Pitter Keller, Auerspergstr. 21, tel: 880552-0. Large cellar bar that serves good food. €

Sternbräu, Griesgasse 23, tel: 842140. Large, popular restaurant with charming courtyard garden in the summer. €€

Stieglkeller, Festungsgasse 10, tel: 842681. Beer hall and garden with lovely views of the city. €€

Weissbierbrauerei, Rupertgasse 10, tel: 76481. Pub brewery in a rustic style; serving good value food. €€

Wilder Mann, Getreidegasse 20, tel: 842138. A favourite with locals and visitors alike. €€

Zipfer Bierhaus, Sigmund Haffnergasse 12, tel: 2843101. Charming beer hall, centrally located. €€

Zum Fidelen Affen, Priesterhaus-

Types of Beer

The most important thing to know about Austrian beer is that no chemicals are used in the brewing process. Beers are brewed in a wide range of styles and with a great deal of skill and care. You might like to sample the following:

Märzen is the equivalent to lager. (Stiegl is the local beer brewed in the city of Salzburg, Kaiser is brewed in Hallein and is the oldest brewery in Salzburg Province.) Augustiner is found only in the Augustinerbräu and a few other taverns. It is the monks' own special brew. It contains no gas and is quite strong.

Weissbier is wheat beer. The yeast is not brewed out from this beer so you can see and taste it. There are three varieties: light, dark and clear.

Keller is Zwickl and this is an unfiltered lager.

Pils is a pale lager with a high alcohol content.

Bock is a special occasion beer. It is only served at Christmas and Easter. It is a dark lager, which is at the top end of the alcohol content. A **Radler** is a shandy made from half lager, half lemonade.

gasse 8, tel: 877361. A traditional tavern serving top-notch food. €€

Restaurants
Austrian
Elefant, Sigmund-Haffner-Gasse 4, tel: 883397. Historic house with Austrian cuisine. €€€
Goldener Hirsch, Getreidegasse 37, tel: 80840. Luxurious hotel restaurant with good reputation. €€€
Humboldt Stubn', Gstättengasse 4–6, tel: 843171. Traditional food with a modern twist and good vegetarian menu. €€
Fleischlaberl, Kapitelgasse 11, tel: 842138. (Lunches only.) Good value home-cooked food and real English tea. €
St Peter Stiftkeller, St Peter Bezirk 1–4, tel: 841268. Worth trying the *Salzburger Nockerl* here. €€€

Italian
Coco Lezzone, Franz Josef Kai 7, tel: 846735. Pasta and fish specialities. €€
Il Sole, Gstättengasse 15, tel: 843284. Good value pizzas and pasta. €€

Nouvelle Cuisine
Ikarus, Hangar-7, Wilhelm-Spazier-Str. 7a, tel: 219777. Exclusive restaurant in hangar surrounding. €€€
magazin, Augustinergasse 13, tel: 84158430. Austrian specialities with a difference. €€€
Riedenburg, Neutorstrasse 31, tel: 830815. Excellent restaurant. One of the city's best. €€€

Heurige (Wine Taverns)
Friesacher Heuriger, Anif 55, tel: 06246-7241114.
Steinlechners, Aigner Strasse 4, tel: 620030.

Bars
Jazzit Musik club, Elisabethstr. 11/5, tel: 876891. A mix of live jazz and DJs, serves warm snacks and cocktails; a mixed crowd.
Bazillus, Imbergstr. 2a, tel: 871631. Trendy bar located on the riverside.
Bellini, Mirabellplatz 4, tel: 871385. Italian coffee house and bar, right next to Mirabell Gardens.
Bricks, Ledergasse 8; www.brick-bar.at. Tucked away off the Linzergasse, great bar staff, younger crowd and pool table.
Diva, Priesterhausgasse 22, tel: 0664-4315317. Gay bar, everyone welcome though.
Murphy's Law, Gstättengasse 33, tel: 842882. Cosy Irish pub serving Irish breakfast, Guinness and a wide selection of whiskies.
Pepe Gonzales, Steingasse 3, tel: 873662. Small lively pub.
Piano Bar Hotel Sacher, Schwarzstr. 5–7, tel: 88977. For those with a sophisticated taste.
Rockhouse, Schallmooser Haupstr. 46, tel: 884914. The biggest and best live music venue in Salzburg.

Cafés
Bazar, Schwarzstr. 3, tel: 874278 (riverside terrace).
Café Fingerlos, Franz-Josef-Str. 9, tel: 874213. Probably the best cakes in Salzburg.
Café Pamina, Judengasse 17, tel: 842338.
Café Sigrist, Grriessgasse 13, tel: 840801. Terrace overlooking river. Attracts customers of all ages.
Coffee Shop, Franz-Josef-Str. 3, tel: 878256. Non-smoking, alternative café.
Glockenspiel, Mozartplatz 2, tel: 841403. Enjoyable tourist trap.
Niemetz Konditorei, Herbert von Karajan Platz 11, tel: 843367. Large, traditional café with outside terrace.
Tomaselli, Alter Markt 9, tel: 844488 venerable old coffee shop with a good selection of cakes.

SPORT AND RECREATION

Information about all recreational and sports activities is obtainable from the Austria Promotion Board and the Salzburg Regional Tourist Authority. For those areas of the Salzkammergut which lie within Upper Austria and Styria contact the Salzkammergut Tourist Authority *(see page 122)*. For on-the-spot information contact the local tourist offices.

MOUNTAIN CLIMBING AND HIKING

The highest peaks, the Grossvenediger and the Grossglockner – the latter actually lies in Carinthia – are accessible only to trained climbers with mountaineering experience. The mountains surrounding Salzburg however attract many amateur climbers.

For the most basic of mountain walks you need stout shoes with an adequate tread and a raincoat. For more ambitious tours it is well worth engaging the services of a trained mountain guide. Guided tours of varying difficulty lasting for several days are offered in the Saalach Valley and conducted walks are offered in the West Dachstein region. The highlight is a two-day tour of the glaciers on the Dachstein. A trekking guide covering the Tennengau holiday region is available locally. Starting from St Martin, ambitious mountain walkers can follow the Gosau Gorge across the Postalm and the Osterhorn group to Puch in the Salzach Valley. In the High Tauern National Park, the park rangers also lead mountain walks.

Useful publications include the *Arno Trail Guidebook*, which covers the 1,200 km (746 miles) of Salzburg's borders and the *Salzburg Hiking Atlas* featuring 10 trekking tours. Both publications are available from the regional tourist board.

CYCLING AND MOUNTAIN BIKING

There are numerous cycle hire agencies throughout the region that now also offer mountain bikes (for a list of addresses, contact the Salzburg Regional Tourist Authority).

Together with the tourist authority they also provide information concerning places where mountain bikes are welcome and where, in the interests of the protection of plant and animal life, they are not.

The **Tauern Cycle Path**, which is clearly marked throughout its entire length, leads along some 300 km (190 miles) of cycle-tracks and quiet roads through a wide variety of landscapes. It winds through the Krimml Waterfalls in the High Tauern National Park to the Pongau and the Tennengau on to Salzburg, continuing through the gently undulating countryside of the Alpine foothills to Passau and beyond.

The route follows the downhill course of the Salzach, so there are no uphill sections. (The Tauern Cycle Path guide can be bought at bookstores or from the Salzburg Regional Tourist

---

Canoeing and rafting

Wild-water sports, including river-rafting in large rubber dinghies take place on the Salzach (starting from Zell am See, Krimml, Taxenbach, Schwarzach and St Johann im Pongau), on the Salzach and the Lammer (starting from Abtenau, Golling, Scheffau, Bischofshofen, Werfen and Kuchl), on the Saalach (starting from Lofer, Unken, Saalbach-Hinterglemm and Saalbach), on the Mur (starting from Tamsweg, Vordertullnberg, and Mauterndorf) and in the Salzkammergut (Bad Goisern, Bad Ischl, Obertraun, Ebensee, Hallstatt and St Wolfgang).

Authority.) The **Pinzgau** section of the Saalach Valley also offers keen cyclists plenty of variety, from easy terrain to circuits for mountain cyclists and a sprint parcours for mountain bikers. The suggested routes for the **Lungau** range from the Mur Valley to challenging mountain tours.

Cycle tours can also be planned through the **Tennengau** section of the Salzach Valley, through the gently rolling hills and moorland of the Alpine foothills around Salzburg, in the Amadé Sports World in Salzburg, in the Pongau and in the Europe Sports Region around Zell am See and Kaprun.

SAILING AND SURFING

The Attersee, Wolfgangsee (the largest and deepest of the lakes) and Mondsee are all great for sailing and surfing, as are the smaller Fuschlsee, Mattsee, Obertrumer See, Wallersee, Irrsee, Grundlsee and Zeller See. You can rent boats and surfboards at reasonable rates on all these lakes .

SKIING

Gastein Valley–Grossarltal: (170 km/106 miles of pistes with 53 lifts and 150 km/94 miles of cross-country tracks). **Amadé Sports World,**

Winter sports for all

Salzburg: consists of the three-valley ski areas Flachau–Wagrain–St Johann and Zauchensee–Flachauwinkel–Kleinarl, as well as the Altenmarkt–Radstadt and Filzmoos–Neuberg ski areas, and the Eben lifts (a total of 320 km/200 miles of pistes with 120 lifts and 220 km/140 miles of cross-country tracks). **Hochkönig Ski area and Ski Maria Alm–Saalfelden**: (160 km/100 miles of pistes with 47 lifts and 200 km/125 miles of cross-country tracks). **Ski area West Dachstein/ Tennengau**: including Abtenau, St Martin, Annaberg, Russbach etc. (195 km/120 miles of pistes, a total of 61 lifts and 260 km/163 miles of cross-country tracks). **Postalm**: (11 km/7 miles of pistes, 9 draglifts, 20 km/13 miles of cross-country tracks). **Obertauern**: (150 km/95 miles of pistes, a total of 26 lifts, 18km/10 miles of cross-country tracks). **Lungau ski region**: (320 km/200 miles of pistes, a total of 40 lifts and 320 km/200 miles of cross-country tracks). **Saalbach–Hinterglemm–Leogang Ski area**: (200km/125 miles of pistes, a total of 60 lifts and 95km/60 miles cross-country tracks). **'Europe' Ski Region Kaprun–Zell am See**: including Schmittenhöhe and Kitzensteinhorn (130 km/81 miles of pistes, 54 lifts and 300 km/188 miles of tracks).

PRACTICAL INFORMATION

Getting There

BY AIR

There are regular flights to Salzburg airport from Amsterdam, Berlin, Brussels, Frankfurt, London, Paris, Zürich and the main Austrian cities. The UK budget airline, Ryanair, flies from Stansted to Salzburg three times a day. There are also a number of charter flights to Salzburg from various points in the UK.

Salzburg International Airport (www.salzburg-airport.com) lies between the Maxglan district of town and the suburb of Himmelreich, some 4km (2½ miles) from the town centre. The airport is linked with the town centre by means of a shuttle bus service as well as by Bus No. 2 and taxis. There are also car rental facilities at the airport, but it may be cheaper to organise hire cars prior to departure.

BY RAIL

Within the international railway network, Salzburg lies on both the north–south axis (Germany–Italy–Balkan countries) and the east–west axis

See the city the old fashioned way by horse-power

(France–Switzerland–Hungary), so it is easily and quickly reached. The train from Vienna to Salzburg takes three hours. Salzburg Central Railway Station (www.oebb.at) is 15 minutes' walk from the city centre.

BY CAR

Travelling to Austria by car from Northern Europe is a long and arduous journey. Drive through Germany and take advantage of the excellent motorway network. Salzburg is about 1½ hours' drive from Munich.

Those driving into Austria must carry a valid driving licence, registration papers and a nationality sticker. Before departure, you should check with your insurance company that you are covered in Austria.

The wearing of seatbelts is compulsory and children under the age of 12 are not allowed on front seats. Speed restrictions in Austria vary: on motorways the maximum is 130 km/hour (80 mph); in built-up areas, the limit is 50 km/hour (30 mph), unless there are signs to the contrary. You can obtain breakdown assistance from SAMTC (Salzburg branch of the Austrian automobile association ÖAMTC),

emergency tel: 120, information tel: 639990. ARBÖ, emergency tel: 123, information tel: 433601.

Parking in Salzburg

Spaces are few and far between in the city centre, and visitors are advised to use the Park and Ride facilities located at the various entry-points to the city.

Getting Around

BY RAIL

Three important railway lines cross the Salzburg region: Salzburg–Zell am See–Saalfelden–Kitzbühel; Salzburg–Gasteiner Tal–Villach and Salzburg–Radstadt–Graz. Some regions, however, are not accessible by rail.

A narrow gauge railway serves the Vöcklamarkt–Attersee and Tamsweg–Unzmarkt sections, where there are also pleasure trips on old-fashioned trains, as well as Zell am See–Krimml. From July to June the Salzburg–Lamprechtshausen section is served by old carriages of the Salzburg Red Electric Railway, tel: 0662-44800/872145.

The Austrian Federal Railways (ÖBB) offer special tariffs for senior citizens, children, families and groups, as well as regional passes and season tickets. Information is available from ticket offices or at www.oebb.at.

BY BUS

The yellow-and-red Federal buses (BB) and private bus companies provide services covering the Salzburg region. For information, tel: 806262.

BY CAR

The Salzburg region is served by a comprehensive road network. Ancient mule tracks leading across the Alps have been transformed into modern mountain roads. There is a toll on the ridge section of the Tauern motorway,

on the ridge section of the Gerlos Road, on the Felbertauern Road, the Grossglockner Road, the Gastein Alpine Road, the Nassfeld Road, Postalm Road and a number of other lesser mountain roads. The Tauern tunnel from Böckstein to Mallnitz is traversed by a railway on to which cars are loaded. Because of the steep gradients, some mountain pass roads are closed to or not recommended for trailer caravans.

Chains are compulsory on some roads during extreme weather conditions in winter. The Grossglockner Road is closed from late autumn until spring. Winter tyres should be carried in case of emergency.

BY BICYCLE

Cyclists will find excellent facilities for touring throughout the region. If you do not bring your own bicycle you will find plenty of rental agencies. Austrian Railways has bicycles for hire at a number of stations *(see also pages 118–9)*.

SIGHTSEEING TOURS

Qualified guides are available for sightseeing tours of Salzburg city. For further information contact information offices within the city *(see page 122)*.

Facts for the Visitor

TRAVEL DOCUMENTS

EU nationals as well as visitors from many other countries, including the US, Canada, Australia and New Zealand, do not require a visa for Austria. Visas are still required by nationals of some Commonwealth countries.

CUSTOMS

Tourists are not required to pay duty on articles brought into Austria for their own personal or professional use. The following items may be imported into the country duty-free: gifts up to a value of €175; 200 cigarettes or 50 cigars or 250g tobacco; 2 litres alcohol (less than 22 percent) and 1 litre alcohol (more than 22 percent). When leaving the country, each traveller over 17 is entitled to the following allowances: 200 cigarettes or 50 cigars or 250g tobacco and 2 litres spirits.

EU citizens are not subject to restrictions as long as the goods are for personal use.

INFORMATION

In the UK: Austrian National Tourist Office, PO Box 2363, London W1A 2QB, tel: 020-7629 0461; fax: 020-7499 6038; www.austria-tourism.at/uk
In the US: Austrian National Tourist Office, PO Box 1142, New York, New York NY 10108-1142; tel: 212 944 6880; fax 730 4568; PO Box 491938, Los Angeles 90049, tel: 310-477 3332; fax: 310-477 5141; 500 North Michigan Avenue, Suite 1950, Chicago/Illinois 60611, tel: 312-644 8029; fax: 312-644 6526. E-mail: info@oewnyc.com; www.austria-tourism.at/us
In Austria: Specific information can be obtained by writing or telephoning the Salzburg Regional Tourist Board or the City of Salzburg Tourist Board: Salzburg Regional Tourist Board, Postfach 1, A-5300 Hallwang bei Salzburg, tel: 0662-6688; fax: 0662-668866; www.salzburgerland.com
City of Salzburg Tourist Board, Auerspergstrasse 7, A-5020 Salzburg, tel: 0662-889870; fax: 0662-8898732; www.salzburginfo.or.at
The Salzkammergut Tourist Authority is responsible for the Upper Austrian and Styrian Salzkammergut. Wiverstrasse 10, A-4820 Bad Ischl, tel: 06132-69090.
Information offices in Salzburg:
Mozartplatz 5, tel: 847-568, 889-87330; fax: 889-87342 (offices open all year round).

For the main railway station, tel: 889-87340 (open all the year round).

SALZBURG FOR CHILDREN

Toy Museum *(see page 33)*. The exhibits are not simply displayed in glass cases, there are also play areas.
Museum of Nature *(see page 35)*. Numerous rooms (such as the Dinosaur Hall, Giants of the Ocean and the Space Hall) with multi-media displays provide an introduction to the history of the earth, mineralogy and the world of plants and animals . Live exhibits in the aquarium and the reptile zoo.
Hellbrunn Zoo. Situated at Hellbrunn *(see page 42)*. If you plan to take children to the zoo as well as the palace and gardens, you will need to allow several hours.

> ### Salzburg Museum Card
> The opening times of the museums vary widely, as do the entrance fees. Some museums and sites outside Salzburg (caves, for example) are only open during the summer. Purchasing the Salzburg Card for one or more days offers entry to many museums for free. Contact the tourist office before you visit for up-to-date information.

ACTIVITIES FOR CHILDREN

Pongau Children's Paradise has a number of holiday facilities with children in mind: children's festivals, pony riding, walks to an old mill, farmhouse visits and a railway trip. Information obtainable from the Salzburg Regional Tourist Authority *(see above)*.
Kinder-Lungauland in the Lungau, provides a week-long programme. Activities range from farmhouse visits and barbecues to a medieval afternoon in a castle and a trip on the Taurach Steam Railway. Information from the Lungau District Association,

Postfach 57, A-5580 Tamsweg, tel: 06474-2145.

Other attractions for children are the wildlife parks in Ferleiten and Strobl, the open-air museum in Grossgmain, the salt mines in Hallein-Dürrnberg, Bad Ischl, Bad Aussee and Hallstatt (*see pages 44, 66, 58, 60 and 69*, the stalagmite caves in Werfen and in Obertraun (*see pages 76 and 70*) and the World of Children Museum in Walchen Castle (*see page 53*).

CURRENCY AND EXCHANGE

The currency in Austria is the euro. 1 euro equals 100 cents. Banknotes are available in denominations of 500, 200, 100, 50, 20, 10 and 5 euros. There are coins for 2 and 1 euro, and for 50, 20, 10, 5, 2 and 1 cent.

The most favourable exchange rate is at banks, and ATMs can be found at many banks. Most international credit cards are accepted in banks, major hotels and restaurants, car hire firms and in many shops.

Banks are generally open Monday, Tuesday, Wednesday and Friday 8am–12.30pm and 1.30–3pm; Thursday 8am–12.30pm and 1.30–5.30pm. The exchange booths at the railway station, the airport, the Festungsbahn and the Altermarkt, as well as the Privatinvest Bank AG (Griesgasse 11) and the Rieger Bank (Judengasse 13 and Alter Markt) are all open for longer, and are also open at the weekends.

SERVICE CHARGES AND TIPS

Although service charges are often included in restaurant prices, it is customary to add 10 percent to the total. Taxi-drivers and hairdressers expect a similar amount.

TIMES

Shops are generally open Monday to Friday 9am–6.30pm and Saturday 9am–5pm. In smaller towns there is a midday break of one or two hours but in Salzburg city most shops stay open through lunchtime.

Shops in Slazburg

Many of Salzburg's best shops are located in the *Durchäser* (passageways) between the streets around the Getreidegasse.

Seifenideen aus Schafmilch (Sheeps' milk soaps), Kaigasse 18–20. A haven of stunningly crafted home made soaps and wonderful smells. Best place for little gifts.

Handwerkskunst in Glas, Sigmund Haffner-Gasse 14. Unique locally crafted glass items.

Katholnigg, Sigmund Haffner-Gasse 16. Specialized selection of classical and jazz music.

Gifts & Things, Judengasse 6. As the name suggests, this is a great place for little gifts and souvenirs.

Vom Fass, Goldgasse. DIY Schnapps; best of Austrian.

PUBLIC HOLIDAYS

1 January; 6 January (Epiphany); Easter Monday; 1 May; Ascension Day; Whit Monday; Corpus Christi; 15 August (Assumption of the Virgin Mary); 26 October (National Holiday); 1 November (All Saints); 8 December (Annunciation); 25–26 December.

POSTAL SERVICES

Post offices are open Monday to Friday 8am–noon and 2–6pm (cashier's desk closes at 5pm). In the larger towns they are also open on Saturday 8–10am or longer. The post office at Salzburg main railway station (Südtiroler Platz) is open 24 hours (although not all services are available around the clock). Stamps are obtainable at post offices and tobacconists.

TELEPHONE

Telephone calls may be made from post offices and from public call-boxes. Most public telephones require telephone cards (sold in various denominations at post offices). Older telephones have a button which must be pressed when the person you are calling replies, otherwise the connection will be interrupted.

Austria's international dialling code from abroad is 43, after which you should dial the area code without the 0 and then the subscriber's number; the code for Salzburg is 0662. To make an international call from Austria, dial 00 + the international code: Australia 61; France 33; Germany 49; Japan 81; Netherlands 31; Spain 34; United Kingdom 44; US and Canada 1.

US Credit Phone Cards: AT&T: 022-903011. Sprint: 0800-200236.

MEDICAL ASSISTANCE

Medical care in Austria is of a high standard. However, not all doctors and hospitals treat patients with health care forms from abroad. Members of state health-care schemes should acquire from their local health department the appropriate health care forms as well as a list of doctors who will treat patients with these

Spoilt for choice with tempting gateaux and cakes

forms. Even if you have completed form E111 (to be replaced in 2005 by the European Health Insurance Card), it is advisable to obtain private medical insurance. Salzburg's main hospital is located at Dr Franz-Rehr-Platz 5, tel: 65800.

Pharmacies are open Monday to Friday 8am–12.30pm and 2.30–6pm, Saturday 8am–noon. There will be a pharmacy open at other times for emergencies. Details of the nearest pharmacy on duty are posted in the window after business hours.

EMERGENCY NUMBERS

Police: tel: 133.
Fire brigade: tel: 122.
Ambulance (rescue vehicle): tel: 144.
Emergency medical service (Saturday, Sunday and public holidays only) for urban and rural areas, tel: 141.

LOST PROPERTY WITHIN SALZBURG CITY

Contact the Federal Police Headquarters at Alpenstrasse 90, tel: 0662-63830.

INTERNET CAFES IN SALZBURG

Bignet Internet Café, Judengasse 5; open daily 9am–10pm.
Internet Café, Mozartplatz 5; open daily 10am–11pm.

ACCOMMODATION

Salzburg offers a wide selection of accommodation for all tastes and budgets. There are, of course, the usual international chains, including Sheraton, Renaissance and Radisson, but there is also a wealth of smaller, more individual hotels. Hotels, hostels and campsites are not just located in the centre of the city. There are also many on the outskirts, should you prefer a little more peace and quiet. The term 'Pension' means 'bed & breakfast'.

The following list is arranged in order of price. €€€ is expensive, €€ is moderate and € is inexpensive. Prices obviously do vary depending on the season. If you are visiting Salzburg either during the Salzburg Festival (mid-July to mid-August) or during Christmas and New Year, it is highly recommended to book accommodation before you arrive.

Altstadt Radisson SAS, Rudolfskai 28/Judengasse 15, tel: 848571-0, fax: 8451781-6, www.austria-trend.at/ass. Overlooking the river in the heart of the old town. €€€

Bristol Salzburg, Markatplatz 4, tel: 873557-0, fax: 87 35 57-6, www.bristol-salzburg.at. Recently renovated luxury hotel right opposite Mozart's townhouse. €€€

Crowne Plaza Salzburg (The Pitter), Rainerstr. 6–8, tel: 88978-0, fax: 878893, www.salzburg.crowneplaza.com. Top hotel near railway station and congress centre. €€€

Die Gersberg Alm, Romantikhotel, Gersberg 3, tel: 641257, fax: 644278, www.gersbergalm.at. Situated on the Gaisberg with wonderful views and an excellent restaurant. €€€

Doktorwirt, Glaserstr. 9, tel: 622973-0, fax: 622973-25, www.doktorwirt.co.at. Friendly hotel with an excellent restaurant in a countryside setting. €€€

Goldener Hirsch, Getreidegasse 37, tel: 8084-0, fax: 843349, www.goldenerhirsch.com. Luxury in the best location. Where Prince Charles always stays when he's in town. €€€

Sacher Salzburg, Schwarzstr. 5–7, tel: 88977-0, fax 88977-551, www.sacher.com. A sister hotel of the world-famous Sacher in Vienna and home of the Sacher cake. €€€

Schloss Mönchstein, Mönchsberg Park 26, tel. 848555-0, fax: 848559, www.monchstein.at. Salzburg's most expensive address. Exclusive hotel with wonderful views of the city and secluded on the Mönchsberg. €€€

Altstadthotel Weisse Taube, Kaigasse 9, tel: 842404, fax: 841783, www.weissetaube.at. Family-run hotel close to Mozartplatz. €€

Arthotel Blaue Gans, Getreidegasse 41-43, tel: 842491-0, fax: 842491-9, www.blauegans.at. Traditional hotel with innovative use of works of art. €€

Austria Classic Centralhotel Gablerbräu, Linzergasse 9, tel: 88965, fax: 88965-55, www.centralhotel.at. Comfortable hotel with tradition and its own brewery. €€

Stadtkrug, Linzergasse 20, tel: 87 35 45, fax: 87 35 45-54, www.stadtkrug.at. Historical house with festival connections. €€

Altstadthotel Amadeus, Linzergasse 43-45, tel: 871401, fax: 871401-7, www.hotelamadeus.at. Small, traditional hotel in pedestrian zone. €€

Astoria Salzburg, Maxglaner Haupstr. 7, tel: 834277, fax: 834277-40, www.astoriasalzburg.com. Situated a short distance from the city centre with good bus connections. €€

Doktorschössl, Glaserstr. 7 & 10, tel: 623088-0, fax 623088-13, www.doktorschloessl.com. Converted castle on outskirts of city. €€

Gästehaus Scheck, Rennbahnstr. 11,

tel: 623268, fax: 623268-22, www.hotel-scheck.com. Comfortable country house-style hotel. €€

Hotel Stein, Giselakai 3-5, tel: 874346, fax: 874346-9, www.hotelstein.at. Centrally located with a wonderful roof-terrace café and bar. €€€

Goldene Ente, Goldgasse 10, tel: 845622, fax: 845622-9, www.ente.at. Small, historical hotel set in the heart of old town. €€

Goldene Krone, Linzergasse 48, tel: 872300, fax: 872300-66. Small, comfortable hotel in one of the main shopping streets. €€

Planning accommodation

The Salzburg Tourist Information Centre on Mozartplatz can help you find accommodation. Mozartplatz 5, tel: 889 87-330. There are also information offices at the main railway station, the park and ride south of the city.

Chiemsee, Chiemseegasse 5, tel: 844208, fax: 844208-70. Cute bed & breakfast in a convenient central location. €€

Elisabeth, Vogelweiderstr. 52, tel: 871664, fax: 871664, www.pension-elisabeth.at. Bright & sunny budget bed & breakfast. Some rooms with own facilities. €.

Haus Wartenberg, Riedenburgerstr. 2, tel: 848400, fax: 848400-5, www.hauswartenberg.com. Traditional hotel with leafy garden. €€

Künstlerhaus, Franz-Hinterholzer-Kai 2a, tel: 0664-3415724, fax: 844568, www.pensionkuenstlerhaus.at. Comfortable B&B situated directly on the river. €

Sandwirt, Lastenstr. 6a, tel: 874351, fax: 874351. Situated directly behind railway station. Good budget bed & breakfast. €

Wastlwirt, Rochusgasse 15, tel: 820100, fax: 820100, www.wastlwirt.com.

Tavern-style accommodation in a house with a *Sound of Music* history. €

YOUTH HOSTELS

Youth hostels are a good budget choice within Salzburg. Out of town they offer some intersting accommodation at reasonable prices. There are six youth hostels in the city, the best two are listed below. Two websites provide general information on most of the Austrian youth hostels: www.oejhw.or.at and www.jgh.at. Catalogues can be obtained from ÖHJV-Salzburg, A-5020 Salzburg, Josef Preis-Allee 18, tel: 0662-8426700.

Jugend & Familiengästehaus Salzburg, Josef-Preis-Allee 18, tel: 842670-0, fax: 841101. Youth hostel catering for families and young people. €

Jugendherberge, Haunspergstr. 27, tel: 875030, fax: 883477, www.junge hotels.at/haunspergstrasse.at. Traditional youth hostel near railway station. €

YOHO Salzburg, Paracelsusstr. 9, tel: 879649, fax: 878810, www.yoho.at. Centrally located friendly and popular youth hostel. €

CAMPSITES

There are four campsites in the City of Salzburg. Comprehensive lists of the numerous good campsites in the Salzburg region can be obtained free of charge from Austria Promotion or the Salzburg Regional Tourist Board (*see page 122*).

FARMHOUSES

There are more than 300 farmhouses offering accommodation in Salzburg. The Salzburg Farm Holidays programme offers farm stays at 30 approved locations. For information contact Panorama Tours and Travel, tel: 0622 883211; fax: 0622 871618; e-mail: petz@panoramatours.at

INDEX

HotelClub
Membership
Discount Card